DONSIDE

ALEX INKSON McCONNOCHIE

with a new Introduction by
Donald J. Withrington M.A. M.Ed.

ABERDEENSHIRE CLASSICS

Republished from the original 1900 edition

James G. Bisset
12 Upperkirkgate
Aberdeen
1985

James G. Bisset
12 Upperkirkgate
Aberdeen
AB9 1BG

British Library Cataloguing in Publication Data
McConnochie, Alex Inkson
Donside — (Aberdeenshire Classics)
1. Don, River, Valley — Description and Travel
I. Title   II. Series
914.12′30481   DA880.D6/

ISBN: 0–948246–01–4

Printed by Fretwell & Brian, Keighley, West Yorkshire

Introduction

The Author

Alexander Inkson McConnochie died in Cricklewood, London, on 7 January 1936 aged 86 years. He had not worked nor resided in Aberdeen for over a quarter of a century and had outlived most, if not all, of his old Aberdeen friends and contemporaries, including his companions on those hill-walks, climbs and cross-country forays in the 1870s–1900s which had been the basis for a series of guides he published at that period on Deeside, Donside, Strathspey, etc. Hence the obituaries at his death tend to be formal, even distant, reverential but not very informative.

McConnochie was born in Speyside in 1850, at Rothes in Moray, and was schooled at Inchberry near Fochabers and at Oyne. He then appears to have remained for some time in the Inverurie area, for he dedicated a book on *Bennachie* in 1890 to Mr Erskine Maitland (1819–1885), agent for the Great North of Scotland Railway Company at Inverurie, "who inspired my boyhood, spent with him at the Back o' Bennachie, with a love of mountains."; indeed, about the age of 16, we are told, he had already "walked across the Highlands from sea to sea". Apprenticed to a law office in Aberdeen, McConnochie first appears in the *Aberdeen Directory* in the edition for 1873–74, based in 74 Union Street (which was to be his business address for some 25 years), and described as "a district manager for the Imperial Union Assurance Company". In the next issue of the *Directory* he was designated "accountant and law stationer" and was so described until he left Aberdeen for Glasgow in 1910 — save that, after 1889, he was entered as a "chartered accountant" (holding an associateship of the English Institute of Chartered Accountants) as well as law stationer: he seems never to have been a member of the Institute of Chartered Accountants of Scotland nor, strange to say, a member of the Aberdeen Society of Accountants. He continued throughout his time in Aberdeen to be the local agent for a number of insurance companies and he held at least one public office — in February 1891 succeeding a local Unitarian minister as secretary of the Aberdeen Fresh-Air Fortnight Scheme for poor children. He was a prominent freemason, helped to edit the *Aberdeen Masonic Reporter* after 1879, and co-edited a new edition of *Craft Masonry* in 1901.

Between 1874 and 1899, as a bachelor, he lived successively at 54 Regent Quay, 36 Union Terrace, 1 East Craibstone Street and 20 View Terrace in Rosemount. But the year 1899 (or perhaps the latter months of 1898) brought major changes: his business address became 115 Union Street; he married; and he bought a family home in the West End, at 76 Devonshire Road (removing in 1908 to a newly-built house at no.88). Mrs McConnochie (whose initials after marriage were C.H.E.M., but whose maiden name I have not discovered) was an artist and is registered as such in the *Aberdeen Directory* in and after 1899–1900: she was to provide the illustrations for her husband's *Donside* reprinted here.

We know surprisingly little about McConnochie, for a man who figured in a group of local *Celebrities of 1885–86*, photographs and drawings taken from an Aberdeen weekly, the satirical magazine *The Northern Figaro*. Here McConnochie is seen as lean, long-faced, clearly tall, dark-haired, with a very full beard and moustache. He had certainly just published his first guide-book, *Ben Muich Dhui* and his Neighbours: *a guide to the Cairngorm mountains*, dedicated to seventeen "Cairngorm friends and and companions . . . in remembrance of many pleasant excursions between Braemar and Spey". The *Figaro* had reviewed it earlier, as the work of a man "of mountaineering celebrity", and that reputation was to be soon extended. On 23 June 1887 McConnochie and five companions climbed Ben Muich Dhui to set off fireworks, in celebration of the jubilee of Queen Victoria: among other notices of that event, recalled afterwards as the day on which the forming of a Cairngorm Club was first discussed, was this one in local dialect by the *Figaro*'s correspondent, the so-called Jeems Sim:

> Aboot twal' o'clock I gaed awa' oot the forth tae see the bonfires and poother deevils an' things they were gyaun tae fire off o' Ben MacDooie. Ye ken that lang leggit chiel McConnochie an' a kyaurn o's neepers were a' upo' the tap o' the hill . . . the sky a westwith turned a' the colours o' the rainbow . . . an' haith I wis terrifeed that some mishanter had ta'en place wi' that halackerit eediet McConnochie, an' that they had a' gane tae kingdom come, minister an' a' thegither.

McConnochie was the secretary of the Cairngorm Club from its incorporation in January 1889 until he left Aberdeen and also the editor of its *Journal* for the first seventeen years of its existence. *Ben Muich Dhui* was clearly intended as a handbook for his hill-walking friends, as were "two interesting little pamphlets prepared . . . in anticipation of excursions of the Cairngorm Club" to *Ben a Bhuird and Ben Avon* and to *Ben Rinnes* in 1891; in the same year came *Lochnagar: its topography, history, traditions, geology and botany*, a more general introduction to Upper Deeside, but nonetheless a serious book for the climber/hill-walker too. The latter obviously paralleled *Bennachie: its topography, historical, traditional and ballad lore, geology and botany* which Wyllie and Son of Aberdeen had also published, apparently with some success, the year before. Bennachie, in particular, (and Lochnagar for the much hardier) were popular hills and the extended accounts of them, with their literary and historical associations, were no doubt intended for a wider audience than Cairngorm Club members and the dedicated hill-walking fraternity in Aberdeen; indeed *Lochnagar* had already appeared in serial form in the *People's Journal* in summer 1891 and had been expanded and revised for Wyllie's publication.

The day of the general guide had arrived, and McConnochie was a ready-made, well-informed and modestly experienced author, noted (in a review of *Bennachie*) for "the attractive and thoroughly readable manner in which he places this storehouse of knowledge . . . before his readers". The next years saw, from McConnochie's hand, a spate of popular guidebooks — to Deeside, Donside, Strathspey and to Inverness and district, as well as collections of photographs and views of these and other areas; there was an expanding tourist market and it needed to be fed. Yet when in 1910 he left for Glasgow, all this publishing activity ceased — for twenty years or more — even though McConnochie still maintained some contacts with the area. An obituary in the Cairngorm Club *Journal* refers to the hill-walking prowess which he still retained in his later years — "he was the one to make the pace, and his endurance was astonishing."

In these later years, his companions were probably the "groups of English friends" mentioned elsewhere as accompanying him on the hills, in the period of his residence in London; his last group of publications, on a related but distinctive interest, suggest also that they were men of a rather different social class — *The Deer and Deer Forests of Scotland: historical, descriptive, sporting* (1923), *Deer Stalking in Scotland* (1924) and *Deer Forest Life* (1932), studies sufficiently serious for him to be elected to a Fellowship of the Zoological Society of London. Having been driven (while he was in the North East) by Lewis Smith, Wyllie, William Jolly and other publishers in Aberdeen to pander to popular interest in the increasingly accessible Highlands, or so it seems likely, once he left the area McConnochie could concentrate on more measured and exhaustive studies intended for a specialist audience. Not that he had not laboured hard at the earlier books, in collecting the information he needed (whether from previous writers or from personal experience in the hills) or in the care and quality of writing he brought to their production; indeed, his reviewers all commented on it. And present-day readers can still appreciate his nicely balanced and well-written accounts, imbued with a finely wrought sense of man's impact on the environment together with his infectious enjoyment of "nature, pure and simple".

The Guide-book

McConnochie's *Donside* is virtually the only modern, or relatively modern, serious guide to the area. While cascades of tourist handbooks on Deeside tumbled from their printers and publishers in the second half of the 19th century and trickled on thereafter, only Lewis Smith's much revised and reprinted *Guide to Donside*, from 1844 onwards, and its effective successor in McConnochie's book, have dealt extensively with their subject. In 1900 our author rightly commented that "at last the Don has begun to claim its proper share of the travelling public's favours", and no doubt what was called this "excellent book on the Don Valley . . . an accurate and interesting history of the country" helped to enhance for some an appreciation of its distinctive character and charm. Yet McConnochie seems to find the 'selling' of Donside to his readers something of an uphill task. It is worth noting the titles given to two collections of photographs to which he contributed introductions: one is merely designated *123 Views of Deeside*, the other he felt obliged to give the persuasive title of *Picturesque Donside*. Again, in *Donside*, McConnochie has felt it necessary to admit the contrast of the glories, for the mountaineer and serious hill-man, of the source of the Dee with the mundaneness of the area in which the Don rises in the borderland Highland of Aberdeenshire and Banffshire: "there is little picturesque in the source of the Don as compared with the Wells of Dee . . . on hill moors whose tame and uninteresting slopes are devoted to the feeding of sheep". But who, among the generality of tourists today, would be quite so dismissive of the grandeur of the country behind Corgarff or of the impressive views from the top of the Lecht?

In truth, Deeside had got a grip on the Victorian imagination which it has taken a very long time to relax. Throughout the 19th century, from the early development of the Pannanich Wells near Ballater to the later foundations of its many hydropathics, Deeside was said to have an especially bracing, healthy and invigorating climate — an obvious attraction to those thousands for whom an emerging medical science had no assured cures in surgery or drugs. It was, in any case, increasingly accessible by road and rail (by rail, indeed, as deep into the hills as Ballater) to those with leisure — even to those who could, in money or in time, only afford a day's excursion into the Highlands. And the whole of Upper Deeside was given a unique attraction by the fact of Balmoral; since the mid-century Queen Victoria had in effect graced it with her 'by appointment' sign. In these respects Donside was clearly ill-favoured, yet McConnochie tried to make the most of what it could offer. In 1850, after all, the Queen had climbed Morven ("on the watershed between Dee and Don" but claimed for Donside as its most impressive mountain) and she had been twice, not only once, to walk in the Woods of Paradise at Monymusk ("need more be said to indicate its beauties?"). Also, there was Feith Well, close to the source of the Dee, which "some had visions of . . . becoming a fashionable resort" — to which remark McConnochie adds, "locally it is held to be in no way inferior to Strathpeffer: certainly it tastes quite as disagreeably as any". What could not be so readily countered was the difficulty in getting to Strathdon: while the railway link from Kittybrewster to Huntly had opened in 1854 and the Alford Valley line, from Kintore via Kemnay and Monymusk to Alford, had been in existence since 1859, various suggestions since then to carry the line further up Donside or to loop around the Correen Hills via Lumsden and Rhynie and join the northern line again near Gartly, had come to nothing. The only way to reach Upper Donside was by coach from Alford, and McConnochie had to admit that there were places there more easily reached from stations on the Deeside line than they were from Alford.

Yet our author was not to be deflected from extolling the virtues of Donside. Bennachie, which offered a very worthwhile climb, was popular, accessible and particularly interesting in its historical and antiquarian associations. There were certainly stretches of Upper Donside which were unequivocally beautiful, even 'romantic' in the contemporary view of romantic beauty — for example, Glen Ernan. And everywhere there were fine buildings, old or more recent: new or reconstructed houses (e.g. Castle Newe, Castle Forbes or Glenkindie House); castellated mansions based on ancient tower houses (e.g. Castle Fraser); tower houses still occupied and much in their original state (e.g. Craigievar Castle); and gaunt, romantic ruins galore of ancient keeps and castles (e.g. Hallforest, Pitfichie, Kildrummy, Glenbucket). It soon becomes clear that *Donside* is much more a historian's guide than McConnochie's *Deeside*, and not only because he finds himself with less to say in descriptions of the river's course or of its geographical surroundings. There was, positively, a good deal more report in *Donside* about the history of the land and its landowners, in direct connection with the buildings (whether ruins or residences) which were still there to be seen by the interested observer. There were also the baron court records of many estates to quote from, often at some length, drawn from the collections printed in the Spalding Club or New Spalding Club publications — something not done in the *Deeside* volume. There were ancient churches to describe, battles and battlefields to recall; there were almost innumerable earth houses, stone circles and sculptured stones to notice. To the present-day reader *Donside* soon begins to feel rather more like a modern guide-book than does *Deeside*, and McConnochie recognises their distinctiveness — "the attractiveness of Donside appeals to others beside the agriculturalist, the fisherman and the mere tourist; the antiquarian, ecclesiologist and the historian will find much to interest them in their peculiar pursuits". Here, then, a new richness awaited the discerning traveller and, perhaps, Deeside could be left to serious hill-walkers and the hordes of "mere tourists"?

McConnochie takes us with him, at a fairly gentle pace, from Seaton and Old Aberdeen to Cockbridge and Corgarff. We find Kittybrewster at its peak of importance as a large railway marshalling yard and a great cattle market, the one now long gone and the other newly doomed. We read that the coming of the railway to Kintore had not brought the hoped-for explosion of feuing-out for residences built by the "merchant princes of Aberdeen", such as had marked the opening of the lower Deeside railway — the village of Blackburn had been a "failure", Kintore received "excursionists" but not rich residenters, Inverurie had only maintained its position as a popular holiday resort for Aberdonians; but on the Alford link, Kemnay had grown very substantially because of the railway and Alford itself was increasingly called upon to cater for summer visitors. We may nowadays think that Craigievar Castle gets too little notice from McConnochie, in contrast with his more extensive accounts of, say, Terpersie Castle or the Castle of Corse. It is also perhaps disappointing that the author, while indicating the positions of many earth houses in the valley, does not describe some at least in the revealing detail which they were given in Lewis Smith's guide. Firmly on the credit side, however, is the attention which McConnochie gives here — far more than in his *Deeside* — to place-names (including farm names such as Hangman's Croft, Gallowshill, etc.) and also his readiness to recount, more freely, the remnant supersitions of the natives in the remoter areas of the Don Valley.

In fact, for all its age, *Donside* remains a very good guide; and, because of its age, it offers us at the same time a welcome glimpse of Aberdeenshire at the turn of last century, highlighting not only the changes that had then occurred but also those which we recognise as having taken place since he wrote. One prospective development we may surely be glad had not, and has not, happened. In the last pages of *Donside*, McConnochie tells us of the iron mines at Allargue, near Corgarff, which had been worked for two seasons in the mid-1860s but were then abandoned because of transport difficulties and costs, and he remarks that prospectors had found plentiful evidence of good iron deposits on the Banffshire side of the hills at the source of the Don and also at the head of each of Glen Ernan and Glen Nochty. What McConnochie did not recall for his readers was that in January 1892, according to a report in the *Aberdeen Free Press* drawn from an article in the *Dundee Courier*, there had been again much talk about opening up the mines — agents for the Duke of Richmond and Gordon had discovered manganese there as well as iron; and the suggestion was being made that, with the help of the expanding tourist market, the ores might now be more easily taken away:

> . . . the whole district has a charm peculiarly of its own and, if once there was a railway to it, it would become a centre of attraction for tourists. They go elsewhere, sometimes for less than half the attractions of Tomintoul. The tourist traffic may be somewhat erratic but it always counts for something. It pays the Highland railway very well, and there is no reason to doubt that it would pay any branch that is constructed to Tomintoul. All that is wanted is the enterprise. Once get a railway and the opening of the mines would follow as a natural result. Then Tomintoul would develop . . . Alford is the point from which a railway should be constructed to be of benefit to the greatest number . . . and should a railway be built from Alford to Corgarff it would be the means of giving an impetus to the linen trade in Corgarff . . .

Such a development might not have seemed, in itself, very threatening to McConnochie and his readers. But a later article (drawn from the same newspaper, the *Dundee Courier*) and its headline might well have done: for there the Upper Donside glens were envisaged as growing into a northern Ebbw Vale and the headline announced that Tomintoul could soon become "A Scotch Merthyr Tydfil"!!

June 1985   Donald J. Withrington
              Senior Lecturer in Scottish History, University of Aberdeen

ABERDEENSHIRE CLASSICS

James G. Bisset hope to publish at regular intervals
the following titles in this series:

G. M. FRASER	Aberdeen Street Names
G. M. FRASER	Old Bridge of Dee and Other Essays
JOHN GRANT	Legends of the Braes o' Mar
ALEX McCONNOCHIE	Lochnagar
ALEX McCONNOCHIE	Ben Muich Dhui and his Neighbours
JOHN HILL BURTON	The Cairngorm Mountains
JOHN MACKINTOSH	History of the Valley of the Dee
JOHN GRANT MICHIE	Deeside Tales
GAVIN GREIG	Logie o' Buchan
G. WALKER	Aberdeen Awa'

Already published, uniform with this edition of DONSIDE is:
Alex Inkson McConnochie, DEESIDE

DONSIDE

BY

ALEX. INKSON M^cCONNOCHIE

ABERDEEN
W. JOLLY & SONS

CONTENTS.

ILLUSTRATIONS

From Drawings by Mrs. A. I. McConnochie.

BALLADS.

[The text is edited and the notes are supplied by Mr. William Walker, author of the " Bards of Bonaccord."]

POPULATION, CHURCHES AND BANKS OF DONSIDE PARISHES.

Parishes, &c.	Popula-tion.	Churches.	Banks.
Alford	1410	E., F., Ep.	N. of S., T. & C.
Auchindoir-Kearn ...	1374	E., F., Ep.	N. of S.
Chapel of Garioch ...	1690	E., F., R.C.	T. & C.
Cluny	1196	E., F., U.P.	N. of S.
Corgarff (quoad sacra)	371	E.	....
Dyce	1343	E., F.	....
Fintray	999	E.	....
Glenbucket... ...	408	E., F.	....
Inverurie	2954	E., F., Ep., R.C., Cong., Wes.	N. of S., T. & C., U.
,, (Royal Burgh)	2549	....	....
Keig	748	E., F.	....
Keithhall-Kinkell ...	822	E.	....
Kemnay	1799	E., F.	T. & C.
Kildrummy... ...	569	E., R.C.	T. & C.
Kinellar	580	E., F.	....
Kintore	2409	E., F.	....
,, (Royal Burgh)	686	....	....
Leochel-Cushnie ...	1146	E., F., U.P.	.. ..
Monymusk	1025	E., F., Ep.	....
Newhills	5526	E., F., Ep.	....
New Machar ...	1432	E., F.	....
Old Machar (Landward) ...	1432	....	....
Oyne	883	E., F.	.. ..
Strathdon	1220	E., F.	T. & C.
Tough	675	E.	....
Towie	939	E., F.	....
Tullynessle-Forbes	975	E.	....

DONSIDE

I.—THE DON

A mile of Don's worth two of Dee,
Except for salmon, stone, and tree.

THE Don is the sixth river in Scotland for length, the seventh for area of basin. It is wholly an Aberdeenshire river, and running in many parts parallel to the Dee, is generally regarded as its "sister" stream. But beyond the fact that both rivers have an Easterly course to the North Sea, mingling with the ocean at Aberdeen, about a couple of miles from each other, and that in certain parts they have a similar picturesqueness, their differences are more considerable than one would expect to find in two rivers having so close a connection. Deeside has long been famed for its scenery and been both a popular and a fashionable resort, but at last the Don has begun to claim its proper share of the travelling public's favours. Till comparatively recently its beauties have been very much ignored—except by anglers, who recognise in the Don the finest trouting stream in Scotland. The general rugged grandeur of the Dee valley is absent, but there are smiling plains and meadows, wooded banks and tree-lined gorges—all cunningly and lavishly commingled as is Nature's way in the Highlands. Indeed one is apt to forget that the Don is by birth a Highland river, rising under the shadow of the Cairngorm mountains.

But the attractions of Donside appeal to others beside the agriculturist, the fisherman, and the mere tourist; the antiquarian, the ecclesiologist, and the historian will find much to interest them in their peculiar pursuits. For the first there need only be named the Bass and numerous Eirde Houses; for the second the Cathedral of Old Aberdeen and the Church of Kinkell; and for the last Harlaw and Kildrummy. Such modern stately piles as Cluny Castle, Castle Forbes, and Castle Newe, stand in juxtaposition to the ruins of the castles of Hallforest, Towie, and Glenbucket; while Keith Hall, Castle Fraser, and Craigievar Castle represent an intermediate class in modern use. In all such buildings the valley of the Don is exceedingly rich; and each has its story, its ballad, or its legend. The commercial element must not be forgotten; the river, for the last few miles of its course, is harnessed to numerous manufactories, some of which are of world-wide reputation.

The Don* rises in the parish of Strathdon, close to the march with Banffshire, its principal head stream touching the county boundary at a point within two-thirds of a mile of Inchrory on the Avon. This burn, Allt an Mhicheil, which rises in Coire Domhain, at an altitude of about 2000 feet, between Carn Cuilchathaidh (2382 feet) and Little Geal Charn (2323 feet), flows at first in a northerly direction before it takes the general Eastward course of the river of which it is generally accounted the parent. There is good evidence, however, that it did not always flow so as to enter the sea by the Don valley, but that it diverged Westward to the Avon at Inchrory, and so its waters found their way to the Moray Firth by the Spey. The name Reidh Allt Mhicheil (the Meadow of Michael's Burn), near Inchrory and within the Banffshire boundary, seems conclusive on that point ; besides there is the testimony of "The Statistical Account" that this burn was at one time actually diverted to turn a mill wheel near Inchrory. Looking closely to the burn, where, at an altitude of 1516 feet, it crosses the drove road connecting Strathdon with Inchrory, one could readily understand that during severe floods its waters might easily be divided between the Don and the Spey ; there are similar such instances at no great distance. A short distance Eastward there is the little tributary Allt Cuilchathaidh from the hill of that name ; still further Eastward is a more considerable burn, Allt Bheannaich, joining the main stream near Inchmore, a sheep farm with the most Westerly house in the strath. Allt Bheannaich springs from Little Geal Charn as Allt Coire Dhomhain, Meikle Geal Charn (2633 feet) as Allt Geal Charn, and Brown Cow Hill (2721 feet) as Meikle Caochan Odhar. The two last named hills, it may be mentioned, separate Strathdon from Glengairn. These head streams flow from the South ; those from the North are more numerous, but individually are of less importance. Allt Clach Mheann and Allt Craig Meann spring from Creag Mheann (2328 feet) ; Allt an Aighean springs from Druim na Cuaich (2135 feet) ; and Allt Reppachie from Tolm Buirich. It will be observed that the name "Don" is not given to any of these burns, but it appears in a disguised form in Coire Domhain and Allt Coire Dhomhain ; it is only when Allt Bheannaich enters the conjoined streams in the centre of the strath, at an altitude of 1410 feet, that map-makers use the river name. Above the confluence with Allt Bheannaich the main stream is called Allt Tuileach ;

* The following list of Scottish rivers, with their lengths in miles and area of basin in square miles, is compiled from a recently published Blue Book :—

1. Clyde,	98·5	1488·0	6. Don,	80·5	515·7
2. Spey,	98·0	1153·5	7. Forth,	64·5	627·9
3. Tweed,	96·5	1680·6	8. Nith,	61.2	496·6
4. Tay,	93·2	2384·4	9. Deveron,	60·0	474·1
5. Dee,	85·2	817·2	10. Findhorn,	56·5	307·2

it creeps almost imperceptibly along a morass known as Feith Bhait. There is little of the picturesque in the source of the Don as compared with the Wells of Dee ; in the latter we find ourselves on the summit-plateau of a great mountain, on gravel and rock at the top of huge corries, where the red deer seek shelter ; in the former on hill moors whose tame and uninteresting slopes are devoted to the feeding of sheep. Yet, separated only by narrow Glen Builg, Ben Avon rears high over all his neighbours in upper Strathdon the huge tors which distinguish him from afar.

There is a popular saying : " He has as many crooks as Don". The "crooks" of Don, particularly for several miles East and West of Inchmore, are so many and bewildering that at a very short distance it is often impossible to tell the real run of the water. The Don, of course, is not without rapids, but taking its length and the altitudes given into account its flow cannot be otherwise than deliberate—of which commercial advantage has been taken, as we have already noted, towards the end of its course.

The Don flows through or along the following parishes :— Strathdon, Glenbucket, Towie, Kildrummy, Leochel-Cushnie, Auchindoir-Kearn, Tullynessle-Forbes, Alford, Keig, Monymusk, Oyne, Kemnay, Chapel of Garioch, Inverurie, Kintore, Keithhall-Kinkell, Kinellar, Fintray, Dyce, New Machar, Newhills, Old Machar, and Aberdeen. Donside can thus boast of three royal burghs—Inverurie, Kintore and Aberdeen. The principal tributaries are :—on the left bank, the Burn of Loinherry, Ernan Water, Water of Nochty, Water of Bucket, Kindy Burn, Mossat Burn, Esset Burn, Burn Hervey, River Ury, and Goval Burn ; on the right bank, Allt a' Choilich, Burn of Tornahaish, Conrie Water, Water of Carvie, Deskry Water, Leochel Burn, Ton Burn, and Tuach Burn.

Besides the hills already named there are several others which should be mentioned here from being so frequently associated with the Don. There are two on the North side of the river, The Buck (2368 feet) and Bennachie (1732 feet)—the latter, with its classic stream, the Gadie, being probably the most popular hill in Aberdeenshire ; on the south, on the watershed with the Dee, there is Morven, Byron's "Morven of snow". But there are numerous less known minor heights, which are so disposed that the valley is very irregular. Here the river has a meandering course through broad fertile haughs ; there it winds through a finely wooded vale ; while in many parts of its course—and even near its mouth—steep banks, narrow rocky gorges, or hill slopes contract the strath to a den. The river has experienced three great floods in comparatively recent times—in 1768, 1799 and 1829—the last being graphically described by Sir Thomas Dick Lauder in his " Moray Floods".

> Ae rood o' Don's worth twa o' Dee,
> Unless it be for fish or tree

is another form of the couplet which heads this chapter. Yet, as already remarked, the Don takes the premier place for trout, but as for salmon, the pollutions from the manufactories and the legal "obstructions" towards its mouth effectually prevent the upper proprietors from reaping the natural harvest of the river. It is possible, however, that they will not always submit to the present state of affairs, and manufacturers may be called upon to conduct their business on slightly different lines. The lower proprietors, with their system of cruives and dykes, have naturally no particular wish for any change which would facilitate the upward run of salmon. The upper proprietors recently stated their case to the Secretary of State for Scotland in the following terms :—

" From the mouth of the River Don for a space of four or five miles, a series of dams exists across the river, by which the ascent and descent of salmon and fish of the salmon kind from and to the sea is seriously interrupted, and can be accomplished only in flood time. This is caused by the fact that the water is diverted from the ordinary channel by means of weirs, and utilised to supply the large manufactories, and the extent to which water has been taken from the river has largely increased of late years, and in the case of the weirs and intakes to Grandholm, Mugiemoss, and Stoneywood, throughout the whole year when the river runs in ordinary volume, practically the whole of the water is taken out of its natural channel. As a result the river bed is dry for a considerable distance below the weirs or dams of these manufactories, and no water, except in flood time, flows over the so-called fish ways or ladders, which presently exists in the weirs ; that the construction of the so-called fish ways in these weirs is obsolete, and even if water did run over them, they are wholly inadequate to allow the free passage to fish in ordinary states of the river ; that, in consequence, the ascending salmon collect in large numbers below the weirs, where they fall an easy prey to poachers, and are caught by grappling hooks and other foul means of fishing, and where, from over-crowding, and laceration caused by snatching and grappling, disease annually breaks out amongst them, frequently killing off hundreds of fish containing millions of ova ; that as a result also of these obstructions the proprietors who have the right to the net fishings adjoining these weirs practically clean the river of salmon ; that even when the river is in a state of flood during the spring months, the nature and height of the so-called fish ways effectually stop the running of the salmon, as they are not capable of ascending them when the river is at a low temperature, and in the autumn season, when the nets are taken off, the present fish ways form an effectual bar to the salmon heavy with spawn, then seeking to ascend, and they have often to be assisted over the weirs by the actual manual labour of the water bailiffs, as many as six hundred having been assisted over in one day ; that there also exists on the river a weir with cruives therein, called the

'Cruives of Don', and that the way in which these cruives, with their objectionable appurtenances, are worked, is grossly unfair to your memorialists, and is wholly in excess of the legal rights of the cruive owners ; that as a result of all this, none of the spring or summer fish, and not nearly the full head of the autumn fish which seek to ascend after the netting terminates, ever reach the waters above the obstructions, and the river's productiveness as a breeding-ground for salmon is seriously impaired ; that your memorialists also suffer heavy pecuniary loss owing to the inferior fishing which the river affords at all seasons, and which is brought about wholly by these obstructions to the free passage of the salmon ; this loss is grossly unfair, as your memorialists pay assessment for the preservation of the fish during the spawning season, but nevertheless have no fishing to repay them for their outlay : that the complaints of your memorialists have been repeatedly made to the Don Fishery Board, but as the owners of the lower fishing, who are benefited by these obstructions are in a majority in the Board, no redress has been obtained from the Don Fishery Board. The obstructions have also been brought before the Fishery Board for Scotland, and reported against very strongly by their late inspector, Mr. Archibald Young, but nothing has been done to remove them ; that the obstructions above complained of could be entirely obviated were the proprietors of the weirs, dams, and cruives compelled to insert in them fish ways or passes of modern construction, and to have a certain amount of water running over these fish ways to the effect and extent of allowing at all seasons and in all states of the river, free passage to the fish ".

So much for the " fish " ; now as to the " tree " of the couplet. It must be allowed that the Don cannot compete with her big sister for the latter ; nevertheless the denudation in recent years of the Don's tree-clad slopes has been carried to such an extent that the realised value of the timber must have been very considerable. Indeed, in many places the valley has been bared to an unsightly extent, and years must elapse before its natural grace and beauty can be restored. Harking back to the first form of the couplet, one may be pardoned for remarking that the Kemnay, and many other quarries, were then unopened.

Another form :—

> The river Dee for fish and tree,
> The river Don for horn and corn,

must not be omitted, referring as it does so pithily to the agricultural richness of Garioch, " the meal girnal of Aberdeenshire ", and the Howe of Alford.

Donside has railway communication to Alford, 29½ miles—by road, 25 only. The Great North of Scotland Railway from Aberdeen (Kittybrewster) to Huntly was opened in 1854 ; the branch from Kintore to Alford in 1859. The Alford Valley Railway, as this branch was called, was leased to, and in 1866 amalgamated with, the Great North of Scotland Railway. Coaches connect Strathdon with Alford and Gartly, but certain Deeside stations are more conveniently situated for particular parts of Donside. The Aberdeenshire Canal was opened in 1807, seven years after the new turnpike, and connected Inverurie (Port Elphinstone) with Aberdeen, remaining in use till the railway took its place. The length of the canal was 18¼ miles, breadth 24 feet, and depth nearly 4 feet. There were 17 locks, each raising the water about 10 feet— the summit level being at Stoneywood, 168 feet above low-water mark. The canal was not a financial success ; the total cost was about £50,000. The bed can still be traced in numerous places.

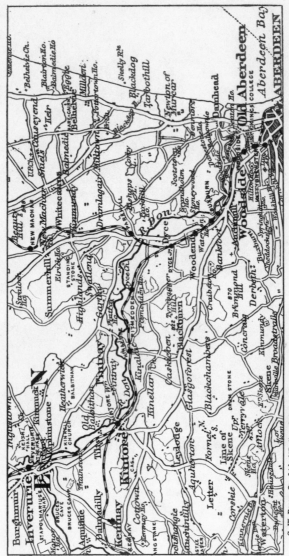

W. JOLLY & SONS, PUBLISHERS, ABERDEEN.

G. W. Bacon & Co., Ltd., W. Strand, London.

[Face p. 15.

II.—ABERDEEN

> Fair city of the rivers twain
>   No child of idle dalliance thou ;
> The silvery borders of thy train
>   Come from the rugged mountains' brow.

F old, Aberdeen, as its name implies, was associated with only one "of the rivers twain"; it was naturally inevitable that it should ultimately annex the South bank of the Don as well as the ancient, if not progressive, cathedral city of Old Aberdeen. The latter has also been known as Aberdon from its intimate relation with the Don ; also as Seaton, and Kirkton of Seaton, from its vicinity to the sea ; while the more familiar Aulton is proof of the antiquity which its big neighbour seems always to have allowed. The Aberdeen of to-day embraces Old Aberdeen, Woodside, Torry, and Ruthrieston, with a population of about 145,000 ; a description of that royal burgh would therefore be out of place in the present booklet. Reference may be made for that purpose to the author's " Deeside " ; here we are more directly concerned with Old Aberdeen and Woodside, and so shall, with all convenient speed, betake ourselves to Donmouth on our pleasant journey up the river, including in this chapter part of Old Machar.

The leading thoroughfare between Aberdeen and Donmouth is King Street, a long street which extends from Castle Street—the square of the city—to Bridge of Don. The Ellon and Peterhead road is a continuation of this street. Old Aberdeen is also connected with the centre of the city by Broad Street (also practically off Castle Street), Gallowgate, Mounthooly, King's Crescent, Spital, College Bounds and High Street ; while there is another route by S. Nicholas Street, George Street, Powis Terrace, and Bedford road to High Street. Two lines of tramways are also available—one from Bridge of Dee to Bridge of Don, *via* King Street ; another from S. Nicholas Street to Kittybrewster and Woodside. The Great North of Scotland Railway has an excellent suburban service as follows :—

Miles.		Miles.	
...	Aberdeen.	2½	Woodside.
¼	Schoolhill.	4¼	Bucksburn.
1	Hutcheon Street.	4¾	Bankhead.
1½	Kittybrewster.	5¼	Stoneywood.
2¼	Don Street.	6¼	Dyce.

The principal buildings in King Street are—on the East side—S. Andrew's (Episcopal) Cathedral, Central Fire Station, King Street Public School, and the Educational Trust Institution ; on the West side — the North of

Scotland Bank, the Medical Hall, the North Parish Church, the East Poor House (in Nelson Street) and the Militia Barracks. King Street runs parallel to the coast line, which is sandy all the way; the Queen's Links are at the Southern end; then there is the Broad Hill (94 feet), on the North of which, stretching to the Don, are the Old Town or King's Links. On the left bank of the river are the Murcar Links, sacred to golf. The Epidemic Hospital abuts on the Queen's Links and the Broad Hill; between that Hill and King Street is Trinity Cemetery, on the North of which is a huge Gasholder, as well as a rifle range. A short distance North of the Militia Barracks is S. Peter's Cemetery — also entered on the North-west from Spital. Between Broad Hill and the Militia Barracks is Gallows Hill (98 feet), where recent gruesome finds indicate its former use. It now serves as a shelter and a convenient spot from which to overlook the ocean and the mouths of the rivers.

The Don enters the sea about three-quarters of a mile East of Bridge of Don. This bridge was built in 1831, at a cost of about £17,000, from plans revised by Telford.

Donmouth. There are five semicircular granite arches, each of about 86 feet span, and it stands at an altitude of about 42 feet above sea-level. The width between the parapets is 26½ feet, doubtless considered ample on its erection, but now quite insufficient for the increased traffic which passes over the bridge. The inconvenient narrowness was recently much in evidence—when there was a suggestion of tramway rails being laid along the road-way in connection with the Seaton Brick and Tile Co.'s Light Railway from Strabathie. There is a Coast-guard Station on the left bank of the river between the bridge and the sea ; in 1851 we are gravely told that "the men at this station, since its commencement, have behaved in a very orderly manner, and appear to attend strictly to their duty ".

In prehistoric times it is said by certain authorities that the Don held directly Eastward from Seaton House and so found an exit to the South of the present mouth. Kennedy ("Annals of Aberdeen") says that probably the Don had in earlier times joined the Dee "in the harbour"—a conjecture so far confirmed by the works of Ptolemy and Richard, who, while duly noting the Dee and the Ythan, ignored the Don on the supposed ground that it was then tributary to the Dee. As to the various mouths of the Don we are on firm ground only from the beginning of the eighteenth century, but we are not without information for half a century previous, and reasonable conjecture as to the position even at an earlier date. The first map on which reliance can be placed is that of Gordon of Straloch, from which we see that about 1650 the Don entered the sea practically at the same point as at present. Some time after that date, however, the river began to turn Southward towards the Broad Hill. The sands on both sides as well as the "spates" which periodically descended from the hills were conducive to changes of outlet. Not that these changes were rapid ; possibly they were almost imperceptible ; yet by the beginning of the eighteenth century the Don had ceased to enter the sea at the point marked on Gordon's map, and had its embouchure, which can still be traced, nearly opposite the Broad Hill. The new channel then began to fill up, and the " white-", as well as the salmon-fishers, found their occupation going. The former indeed forsook Donmouth altogether, and the heritors of the fishings of Nether Don resolved to send the river back to its 1650 course as it had " deviated from its ancient channel, whereby the fishing was like to have been sunk and lost ". They accordingly entered into a contract with one of their number, Professor James Gregory, M.D., of King's College, to restore the old channel.

The task was finally accomplished on 1st June, 1727, nature that day assisting the Professor by a " great speat". Gregory built a dyke or bulwark, 430 yards long, to keep the Don in an Eastward course, in the erection of which the workmen came across the remains of a previous dyke " much slapped and broken ", which is suggestive. It would appear that Gregory had conducted the operation at a profit of £55, which he generously " mortified " as the nucleus of a fund for " decayed " salmon-fishers. The Nether Don heritors made in 1822-4 an important addition to the 1727 dyke, extending it 262 yards seaward. Their fishings, it should be mentioned, extend 2640 yards up the river ; from the East end of the dyke or breakwater to the "new" bridge, 1006 yards ; new to old bridge, 660 yards ; and old bridge to a march stone opposite Seaton House, up to which the tide flows, 974 yards. The sea fishings extend 2085 yards and 2047 yards South and North respectively--stones on Broad Hill and Berryhill marking these boundaries.

The first Stake Net placed upon the coast of Aberdeenshire was erected about 1822, by the proprietor of Seaton, immediately to the North of the Nether Don sea fishings. The courts having decided that such Nets were not forbidden by law, the Nether Don proprietors were compelled to follow, in self-defence, the example thus set. The present proprietors of the Nether Don and Sea Fishings are :—Shipmaster Society of Aberdeen, Representatives of Duncan Forbes, Hogarth & Co., Mrs. Jane Gray, Representatives of Mrs. Margaret Leith, Rev. Duncan G. Mearns, Henry W. Knight Erskine, Mrs. Margaret I. Dundas, Trustees of Misses Leslie, George Davidson, George A. Walker, and William R. Paton.

Small vessels formerly sailed up the Links by the channel which was closed in 1727, loading and unloading at the Brickworks. The white-fishers seem to have followed the Don in the change which began after 1650 ; according to the evidence of an aged witness on 12th Oct., 1796, " There were houses of white-fishers which he remembers the building of, upon the end of the Seafold to the North of the Ramhillock, and they were

seven in number ; and these fishers carried on the white-fishing
business at sea for about two years ; that at this time the river
ran in a course called Old Don, past the Old Town brick kilns,
and was discharged into the sea near to the Broadhill ; in
which tract there were many shoals, whereby these fishers could
only go to sea, and return at or near to flood tide, and was so
inconvenient for their business that they abandoned the station
and their houses altogether ; that the said old course was so
long of filling up that he remembers salmon having gone
up it and fallen into holes, and been taken after the tide
retired ".

The term " *Old* Don " is exceedingly suggestive, especially
when considered in connection with Parson Gordon's " Description ". The inference is that while the Don flowed Eastward
about 1650, as shewn in Straloch's map, yet at a still earlier
date it had entered the sea by the mouth which became closed,
for the second time at least, on 1st June, 1727. The Parson,
who was son to Straloch, in his " Description of Bothe Touns
of Aberdeen " (1661), refers to a long narrow loch called
" Cannowswett's Pot ", which it was affirmed was at one time
part of the channel of the Don.

A map, dated 1746, shews Gregory's "bulwark", and has
this note :   "A bulwark built by the citizens to divert ye
current more easterly for better Fish ". The most interesting
and accurate map published while Gregory's diversion was
fresh in men's minds, is that of Peter May, dated 1756. It
shews not only the Don entering the sea as Gregory altered it,
but the previous channel is also indicated. The " Lakes or
Ponds of Water commonly called Canno Sweets Potts", are
marked on the right bank of the old course.

The amenity of the Old Town Links is not improved by these
"Potts", nor by the meandering stream which flows Northward to
the Don from the neighbourhood of Cow Hillock, a very gentle
eminence which, found to be in the way of volunteer shooting
competitions, has suffered accordingly.   The streamlet first
appears as (we give the names from the Ordnance Survey maps),
Canny Sweet Pots ; then it becomes Banstickle Burn, entering
the river, however, as Tile Burn, after having received Powis
Burn from the left. At High Water the Don is forced some
distance up Tile Burn.

Brig o' Balgownie is about a third of a mile Westward from
Bridge of Don.   Between the bridges, on the North bank, are
a little hamlet, Cot Town, and Don Mills, erected as a distillery
in 1798 ; the South bank would form an excellent walk were
the foot-path in better order.   The small island between the
bridges was of old known as Allochy. It should have been
stated that the Don is a "navigable" river ; previous to 1831
small vessels came up to Don Mills and discharged
their cargoes.   The river makes a brave show at High
Water between the bridges ; at Low Water it is less pre-
sentable.

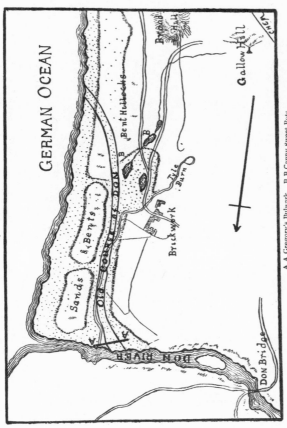

A A Gregory's Bulwark.   B B Canny Sweet Pots.

Donmouth—from Peter May's Map (1756).

> Brig o' Balgownie, wight is thy wa',
> Wi' a wife's ae son on a mare's ae foal,
> Down shalt thou fa'.

The antiquity and the Byronic associations of this bridge,
coupled with the beauty of the scene, have rendered it famous,
and distant visitors to Aberdeen almost
Brig o' Balgownie. invariably make a pilgrimage to this ancient
gothic arch. It made a great impression on
Byron (" Don Juan ", Canto x. 18, with foot-
note) :

As " Auld Lang Syne " brings Scotland one and all,
    Scottish plaids, Scottish swords, the blue hills, and clear streams
The Dee, the Don, Balgownie's brig's *black wall ;**
    All my boy feelings, all my gentler dreams.

*The Brig of Don, near the " auld town " of Aberdeen, with its one
arch, and its black, deep salmon stream below, is in my memory as
yesterday. I still remember, though perhaps I may misquote, the
awful proverb which made me pause to cross it, and yet lean over it
with a childish delight, being an only son, at least by my mother's side.

The poet does misquote ; for "black wall" read "wight
wall".

The prediction which heads this section is attributed to
Thomas of Erchildoune, and is familiar in Aberdeen, where
Byron spent some of his youthful years. The Rhymer, as will
be seen as we advance up the river, did not confine his
prophecies to the lower part of the Don.

The height of the arch is $34\frac{1}{2}$ feet, with a span of 67 feet ;
the carriage way is only $10\frac{1}{2}$ feet ; the approaches, though
somewhat improved in recent years are as inconvenient as is
generally the case with old bridges. Its erection, both as to
founder and date, is somewhat obscure. Henry Cheyne, of
the Cheynes of Inverugie, the thirteenth Bishop of Aberdeen, a
nephew of Comyn, Earl of Buchan, who was killed by Bruce at
Dumfries, had to seek refuge for a while in England owing to
having espoused the cause of his uncle. On the bishop's
restoration—and possibly at the instigation of the King—he
built the bridge probably about 1320, from the accumulated
revenues of his see during his absence. Be that as it may,
Sir Alexander Hay, to whom the bridge was latterly so much
indebted, states (1605) that it was built at the orders and
expense of the Bruce. Between the dates mentioned the even
then ancient structure had become " ruynous ", and it was
found to be no easy matter to procure funds for its repair, but
the gallant knight came to the rescue for all time. He left
certain portions of land, then of the yearly value of £27 8s. 8d.
Scots = £2 8s. $5\frac{1}{2}$d. sterling, the accumulated funds of which
amounted in 1872 to £23,153 7s. 8d. The Trustees of the
fund are the Town Council of Aberdeen, who were enjoined to
divert the bequest " to no other uses, as they shall answer to
God at the last judgment ". Nevertheless the surplus funds

have been put to good use ; the cost of the new bridge (1831) was thus defrayed, not to mention other structures which have largely benefited therefrom.   A tablet on one of the buttresses on the South-east wing wall thus commemorates the "mortifica- tion " : "A S H Anno, 1605, Dominus Alex. Hay, Clericus Registri Ex innato in rempublicam amore £27 8s. 8d. Scoticus exquibusdam ad Aberdoniam agellis quotannis memorandos huic fabricæa sustendandæ dedicavit ".

The river, seen from the bridge, is a dark sullen stream, over 20 feet deep at low tide, but the scenery to the Westward is charming.   The steep and wooded Braes of Don here confine the left bank of the river, noted spots being Black Nook (on the North side of the bridge), Tam's Hole, Lovers' Loup, a weir, and Devil's Rock—all suggestive names.   The depth at Black Nook is said to be 33 feet, the deepest "pot" in the river : "deep as the water is at this place, many a good salmon I have assisted to take out of it, and many a hundred has my father and grandfather taken out of it before my day, and now (1851), I may say, it is a barren pool when compared with what it was then ".   "Tam's Hole" should be (Dr.) Thom's Hole— so called from an erstwhile resident at Braehead Cottage in the immediate vicinity.   Lovers' Loup refers to two lovers who quarrelled here and were drowned—the swain losing his life in attempting to save his sweetheart.   As for the Devil's Rock— the only explanation is that, as usual, when the locality itself cannot supply a name for a natural curiosity there is always his Satanic majesty as a reserve.   The left bank here has much attraction for artists ; the view embracing the cathedral spires is probably the finest.

North of the bridge are Denmore and Scotstown, both finely wooded ; Perwinnes Moss lies between them.

Old Aberdeen did not come empty-handed into the greater Corporation.   Its principal asset we consider to be the Commonty of Perwinnes, called also Scots-

Perwinnes.

town Moor, concerning which Mr. Alexander Walker, LL.D., recently published a neat booklet.   The Commonty, which is noted for its botanical wealth, lies in the parish of Old Machar, about three miles from Castle Street, being thus within easy reach by tramway.   "It has not been kept as it has without a struggle.   It has been coveted by neighbouring lairds, and *sans doute*, could each of them have proven how much was his, it would have been parcelled out and divided long ago.   En- croachments have been and still are being made, but the people of Aberdeen have still a grand possession there, and it will· be their own fault if one other rood of it is lost ".   Mr. J. W. Davidson, Depute Town Clerk of Aberdeen, states in his "The Common Moss and Freedom-Hill of Old Aberdeen ", (1896) ;   "The moss of Perwinnes, called also the Commonty of Perwinnes, is at present about 229 acres in extent, but in former times it included portions of land now enclosed within

Brig o' Balgrownie

the fences of Perwinnes. The Moss, or Commonty so called, includes the moss portion at the North end, which has yielded peats and fuel for the exclusive use of the feuars at Old Aberdeen, and the Corsehill, South of the peat moss, which has provided common pasture and feal, divot, etc., for the feuars in common with the proprietor of Perwinnes. The public have been in the custom of walking all over the Commonty. While the Bishop granted rights of common pasture and other servitude rights, there has been no grant to any one of a right of property or of commonty in the land in question, and there is no Commonty in the proper legal sense of the word. The land, although not properly a Commonty, continues to be referred to as "the Commonty.'"

Old Aberdeen was, and indeed may still be considered, a long straggling town, built mainly on both sides of the old Buchan road. Notwithstanding its amalga-

Old Aberdeen. mation with its big neighbour it is unaffected by the bustle of modern towns ; indeed its very atmosphere seems to partake of the dignified leisure and academic calm which so well become a Cathedral and University City. It is said to have been of considerable importance so early as the end of the ninth century, but it was never a place of commerce or manufacture, the brewing of good ale excepted. David I. translated the see from Mortlach (Dufftown) to the Don, granting "to God and the blessed Mary, S. Machar, and Nectarius, Bishop of Aberdeen, the haill village of Old Aberdeen". A bull of Pope Adrian IV., dated 10th August, 1157—the first authentic writ connected with the Bishopric of Aberdeen, *vide* Munro's "Records of Old Aberdeen" published by the New Spalding Club—confirms all grants to the "church of Aberdeen" made by the Kings of the Scots. Then follows a charter by William the Lion confirming the gifts of David I., while James IV. grants two charters—the first in 1489, creating Old Aberdeen a free Burgh of Barony, and the second in 1498, confirming previous rights and of new creating it a Burgh of Barony. The glory of Old Aberdeen is its Cathedral. Situated on high ground overlooking the Don, the gray pile with its graceful twin spires, visible for a considerable distance above the trees, is a structure well worthy of attention both by ecclesiologists and antiquarians. Occupying the site of a former church, it was begun in 1378, but not finished till 1552 ; the quality of the workmanship and elegance of design—and, it may be added, possibly the poverty of the district—explain the long time taken in building. It suffered much at the Reformation ; "so violent was the zeal of that reforming period against all monuments of idolatry, that, perhaps, the sun and moon, very ancient objects of false worship, owed their safety to their distance". The Nave only of the ancient building remains ; the Transept and Choir, with the great Eastern Tower, which had a height of 150 feet, are no more—the former can however be traced. The Bishop's Palace stood at the East end, but no trace of it is now visible. The Nave, which is 135 feet long and 65 feet broad, is in use as the Parish Church, and the "heritors" and others have thoughtfully enough restored and improved it. The ceiling is ornamented with panels on which are the arms and titles of the Princes, Prelates, and Nobles who had contributed to the expense of the building. The names of the Scottish Sovereigns from Malcolm II. to Queen Mary, as well as those of the Bishops of the Diocese, are also inscribed. Several windows have been fitted with exquisitely stained glass, some of them as memorials.

The first Cathedral on the present site dates from 1163, and was indebted to Bishop Matthew Kyninmond for its erection. Bishop Cheyne, of bridge fame, did not think it sufficient for the Diocese and so he pulled it down, building one more glorious in its stead. But the latter soon shared the fate of the former, and Bishop Alexander Kyninmond began the erection of the present structure. Its architecture belongs to the Norman style, but the Nave, windows, and marriage porch are Gothic. Bishop William Elphinstone, however, was its greatest benefactor. The two Western spires, about 113 feet in height, were completed by him ; he also finished the Eastern Tower which he furnished with a peal of fourteen bells. Cromwell's soldiers are said to have been responsible for the fall of the Tower, when removing stones for the fortification of Castle Hill in Aberdeen.

"A curious legend is related to account for the origin of the See of Aberdeen. According to it Machar or Macarius, along with twelve companions, received instructions from Columba to wander over Pictland, and to build his cathedral-church where he found a river making a bend like a bishop's staff. Such a bend was found in the Don at Old Aberdeen. S. Machar's Cathedral, built beside it, keeps alive the saint's memory. In the neighbouring grounds of Seaton is S. Machar's Well. Though now neglected, it was honoured in former times, and its water was used at baptisms in the Cathadral".—(Mackinlay's "Folklore of Scottish Lochs and Springs".)

So early as the reign of Malcolm IV. there was a seminary of learning in Old Aberdeen which, among other good deeds, Bishop Elphinstone improved into a University. He applied through James IV. to Pope Alexander VI., who in 1494 granted a Bull instituting a University dedicated to S. Mary, but the college being under the patronage of the King was called King's College. It was united in 1860 with Marischal College and University, the combined Colleges being called Aberdeen University. King's is now mainly devoted to Arts and Divinity, Marischal to Medicine and Law. The library attached to King's College is a very fine one and contains about 100,000 volumes ; the Chapel, a beautiful and interesting building, has recently been restored. Adjoining the Chapel is a Tower surmounted by a crown with a cross, giving it an elegant as well as a pro

The Don near Seaton

minent appearance. The College Crown and the Cathedral Spires are the outstanding architectural features which, at a distance, give character to and distinguish the ancient city. Aberdeen, and Scotland generally, may well be proud of the famous men who have borne sway over the ancient University in High Street of Old Aberdeen ; its Chancellors, Rectors, Principals and Professors have embraced men of world-wide reputation, and they have sent forth graduates to all parts of the earth who have done credit to their Alma Mater.

Bishop Elphinstone also founded the Snow Church in Spital, which was dedicated to S. Mary *ad nives*. The Church has disappeared, but the burial ground remains.

Near the College, and on the opposite side of the street, are two towers at the entrance gateway to Powis grounds. These attract not a little attention, both from their resemblance to Mahommedan minarets and their apparent antiquity. They date, however, only from about 1830.

The Town House faces the North end of High Street at the point where that thoroughfare forks— on the right, by Don Street, to Balgownie Bridge ; on the left, by Chanonry, to the Cathedral. The Cruickshank Botanic Garden, now in process of formation in Chanonry, is a worthy memorial of the late Mr. Alexander Cruickshank, LL.D., and of his sister, who so generously presented it. Seaton House overlooking the Don, is a short distance to the North from the Cathedral ; Tillydrone is to the Westward. The latter is a little conical mound (129 feet), and served as a Mote Hill when the Bishops ruled in old times.

Kittybrewster was the original terminus of the Great North of Scotland Railway, and is still an important station. Here **Kittybrewster.** are large goods marshalling yards, engine shops, stores, etc. When the railway was first extended into the city, the line followed pretty much the bed of the old canal to Waterloo Quay—now that portion is reserved for local and harbour goods traffic, passenger trains and through goods being sent to the Guild Street terminus *via* Hutcheon Street and Schoolhill. Kittybrewster is noted for its cattle sales. The road forks just beyond the station, the left hand route being the old Turnpike (between which and the railway lies Woodside) ; the more modern and convenient thoroughfare is on the right.

Woodside, a collection of villages on the North road, was constituted a Police Burgh in 1868, having then a population of **Woodside.** about 4,800. The main thoroughfare is now known as Great Northern Road, and extends from Powis Terrace, Kittybrewster, to the city boundary at Scatter Burn. This long street was formerly known as Wellington Street, Hadden Street, and Barron Street. Woodside is quite a modern name and embraces Tanfield, Cotton, Middlefield and Old Cruives ; it was also called Printfield from its calico printing works. Tanfield was formerly part of the lands of Cotton and was granted on lease of "three lives, when any one of which falls, the proprietor is obliged at the desire of the tacksman to renew it and insert another life upon payment of £25 (the yearly tack duty), by way of fine, and so on for ever". There is no tradition of a tannery in this neighbourhood; but it is believed to have derived its name from having been at one time the residence of of a tanner. Cotton forms the central portion of Woodside; it is most probably a corruption of Cot-town, there being mention of a Gordon of *Cottoune* so early as 1625. The estate of Wood side was formerly known as Smithyhaugh (the name Smith-field is still in existence), Cruives, and latterly Old Cruives. It is called Croffs in an Aberdeen charter dated 1440, and Crwuys in a charter by James III. dated 1465. The names indirectly shew the importance and value of the river salmon-fishings even in ancient times. It is stated on record in 1664 concern-ing these cruives, then lately built and renewed, near the mouth of Cruive (now Scatter) Burn, that the Earl of Mar with certain other noblemen and free-holders upon Don, with about 2500 horse and feet, convene at Kintore and Hallforest for breaking down the same". Which the Earl accordingly did. He might have removed the Don itself with such an army; but perhaps the scribe added a cypher to the number! The cruives were thereafter constructed lower down the river at Rapahana, opposite Gordon's Mills, where they still remain, notwithstand-ing the growls of the upper proprietors of the Don Valley. The Cruive Salmon Fishing belongs to :—Alex. Hadden & Son, Representatives of Duncan Forbes, George Gray's Trustees, Earl of Kintore, William R. Paton, Trustees of the late George G. Hill, and Alex. Pirie & Sons, Limited.

The estate of Woodside embraces the site of the earlier industries—the Waulk Mill, the Snuff Mill, the Bleachfield, Calico Printing and Cotton Mills, the latter known as Woodside Works. The firm of Gordon, Barron & Co. came into existence in 1785, "for carrying on the business of a printfield and of manufacturing linen and cotton clothes, and cloths of linen and cotton mixed for printing"; it employed about 1000 workmen. The younger worklads were accommodated in a rather preten-tious building, known as The Barracks, which attracts attention among its surrounding trees on the river-side, a little to the West of the Works. This large and important firm, which was the second to introduce cotton mills into Scotland, collapsed after an existence of nearly 80 years. The Works were tenant-less for some time, but now form part of the premises of Alexander Pirie & Sons, Limited, Paper Manufacturers. Woodside House is situated between the Works and the Barracks.

On the right bank of the Don, at the South-east end of the Cruive Dykes, are Gordon's Mills; the upper premises are in the occupation of Alexander Hadden & Sons, woollen and carpet manufacturers, the lower are leased by the Donside

Paper Co., Limited. These mills are connected with Woodside by Hayton Road. Paper was first made here in 1696 ; in 1703 a cloth manufactory was in operation.

On the opposite bank of the river from the Donside Paper Co.'s works are Kettock's Mills (corn, &c.), North of which are Balgownie Lodge and Balgownie House, finely situated mansions. Balgownie was for some time known as Fraserfield.

The Board School in Woodside had originally the distinction of being the second largest in Scotland. The Anderson Free Library, the gift of the late Sir John Anderson, a distinguished son of Woodside, is a handsome building containing about 10,000 carefully selected volumes, and a portrait of the donor painted by Sir George Reid. Byron lived for a short time in Woodside, in the house then numbered 177 Barron Street, with his nurse, Agnes Gray (Mrs. Alexander Melvin).

The estate of Hilton, adjacent to Cotton and Middlefield, was anciently called Caponston, Capriston, and Capraston, and was noted for its granite quarries, most of which are now exhausted. The mansion house dates from 1729, but has been enlarged and improved on several occasions, and is now a pleasant residence. Hilton was held in 1561 from the Bishop of Aberdeen for a yearly payment of five merks and eight pence (Scots). Latterly it came into the possession of the Caskieben Johnstons, but was sold by the ninth baronet in 1873 for £20,000. Near the house is a Standing Stone called the "Lang Stane" ; on the North side is Stewart Park, the most recently acquired Public Park of the city.

Grandholm Works, on the North side of the river, opposite Woodside, is one of the most important manufactories in the North of Scotland. The Works are connected with Woodside by means of a private bridge over the Don erected by the firm of Leys, Still, & Co., afterwards changed to Leys, Masson, & Co., about 1810. This firm, formed in 1749 for the manufacture of linen thread and cloth at Gordon's Mills, entered in 1792 into an arrangement with the proprietor of Grandholm for a bleach-field, and latterly mills, on his estate, and at once proceeded to make the present Mill Lead. It is over a mile long, extending from a point West of Downie Hill, and re-entering the Don immediately below the Cruive Dikes, and as in many places rock had to be cut through, it was an expensive undertaking. At the intake there is a ledge of rock across the river which, in 1805, was so improved by Leys & Co., that their water supply was considerably augmented. A law suit on the question of water-rights ensued ; it lasted over twenty years, and is believed to have cost Leys, Masson, & Co. about £30,000. The Works were very prosperous, and the collapse of the firm in 1848 was quite unexpected. They were re-started under new management in 1850, but came to grief again in 1854. In 1859 the plant was purchased by J. & J. Crombie of

Cothal Mills, who by and by transferred their whole business to Grandholm. The firm, now J. & J. Crombie, Limited, employs about 1000 hands, and produces cloth (particularly coatings, suitings and tweeds), which cannot be surpassed for quality.

The Grandholm Lead flows through Persley Den. This " Den " is a picturesque tree-lined gorge practically unknown to most Aberdonians. A saunter along the North bank from Balgownie Bridge to Persley Bridge will reveal much of the beautiful as well as the useful to the observant pedestrian. The Den is a shady retreat, where no scorching sun penetrates, and so the trees grow more to length than to girth ; but the place is a paradise of greenery—a natural cloister, moist, cool, and secluded. The banks of the Lead are luxurious with ferns, grasses, and flowers, and the fat damp soil is carpeted with leaves of heavy hue, from dark bronze to the lemon yellow of the elm, but the rich copper of the beech predominates.

The principal estates, with their owners, in Old Machar, are —Wester Hatton, Society of Advocates in Aberdeen ; Balgownie Lodge, Trustees of the late John Crombie ; Grandholm Mills, J. & J. Crombie, Limited ; Danestone, James F. Crombie ; Balgownie, Trustees of the late Duncan Forbes ; Murcar, Marriage Contract Trustees of Captain and Mrs. Charles B. Fisher ; Seaton, Malcolm V. Hay, and his curators ; Scotstown, William B. Moir ; Grandhome and Persley, William R. Paton ; Persleyden, Theodore Crombie and others ; Denmore, Thomas Adam ; and Parkhill, Testamentary Trustees of Alexander Gordon.

III.—ABERDEEN TO KINTORE

We love thee well, thou beauteous Don,
   That flowest round our home ;
And oft our hearts to thee revert,
   Wherever we may roam.
We think upon thy tiny waves
   That sparkle to the sun,
And on thy haughs, where oft our feet
   In infancy have run.

THE Alford and Strathdon direct turnpike leaves the city *via* Queen's Road at Sunnyside, Hazelhead, but keeps at some distance both from the railway and from the river. Proceeding through Skene, it first touches the railway at Tillyfourie and crosses the Don at Bridge of Alford. We therefore continue our upward journey by the road from Scatter Burn, the West boundary of the Woodside division of Aberdeen. There is also a road on the left bank of the Don, but it is convenient for local purposes only. In this section of our excursion it passes through the parishes of Old Machar, New Machar, and Fintray ; the North road traverses Newhills, Dyce, Kinellar and Kintore. The railway stations to Dyce, inclusive, will be found on page 15 ; to which should be added in this section :—

Miles (from Aberdeen.)	Miles (from Aberdeen.)
8¼ Pitmedden.	7½ Parkhill
10½ Kinaldie.	11½ Newmachar.
13¼ Kintore.	

The principal estates, with their owners, in this important parish are :—Derberth, &c., Mrs. Aberdein ; Jessiefield, John Adam ; Kirkhill, Lady Carnegie ; Fairley,

Newhills   Testamentary Trustees of the late James G. M. Byres ; Cloghill, Major Robert Campbell ; Gateside, Professor Chrystall ; Bonnymuir, James Collie ; Walkermill, &c., John C. Couper; Old Whitemyres, Mrs. Isobel Donald and Misses Gray ; Harthill, Peter Ferries and William A. Hay ; Sheddocksley, Captain George C. Fraser ; New Park, Mrs. Barbara Gibson; Bucksburn, Miss F. C. Jelf Sharp and William Ritchie ; Little Clinterty, John Godsman ; Whitemyres, Trustees of Peter Grant and Weaver Incorporation ; Smithfield, Mrs. Jessie Hall ; Bellfield, George Collie ; Stoneywood or Auchmull and Sclattie, Malcolm V. Hay and his curators ; Denhead, John Imray and Isabella Imray ; Kingswells, Trustees of the late Andrew Jopp ; Springhill, Trustees of the late James Matthews ; Muirfield, Peter

Milne ; Willowpark, Alexander Mitchell ; Gillahill, Alexander
Porter ; Mastrick, Trustees of the late William Murray ; Old-
mill, Parish Council of Aberdeen ; East Middlefield, Repre-
sentatives of the late John Philip ; Hillhead of Pitfodels, William
Pyper ; Upper Rosewell, The City of Aberdeen Land
Association, Limited ; Hazelhead, Representatives of the late
Donaldson Rose ; Craibstone, Alexander Scott's Hospital ;
Kepplehills, Rev. James Smith, LL.D. ; Tulloch, University of
Aberdeen ; Caskieben, James Stephen ; Waterton, Alexander
Pirie & Sons, Limited ; Sclattie, University of Aberdeen ;
Mugiemoss, Charles Davidson & Son, Limited ; Grove, The
Grove Cemetery Company, Limited ; and Redpool, University
of Aberdeen.

Scatter Burn crossed, the first point of interest on the right
is Grove Cemetery, close to which the Don is crossed by Persley
Bridge, a granite structure of recent erection. On the left
bank of the river is Persley Quarry, noted for its fine granite ;
almost opposite, on the right bank, are the more prominent
Dancingcairn Quarries. The latter have been successfully
worked for over a century, London being at one time the great
market. The number of granite quarries has increased within
recent years—even the refuse is now utilised. It may now be
said that Nether Don is as rich in stone as in manufactures.

Newhills, according to "Macfarlane's Geographical Collections", is "miserably divided with mountains" ; one is not so
very much surprised to see a writer of 1725 speaking thus
disdainfully of hills. But to read in Smith's "New History of
Aberdeenshire" (1875) that its chief topographical feature, the
Brimmond Hill, is "a large worthless undivided common of between five and six hundred acres in extent" is really astounding.
Why "worthless"? The hill is a popular holiday resort, and
the right to climb its rough slopes is much valued by the
public. Brimmond has an altitude of 870 feet, and was a
station of the Ordnance Survey in 1817. In former times it
served as a site for a beacon "to give notice to the countrie
people of the approtcheing of foran enemies", according to a
minute of the Town Council of Aberdeen, dated 22nd August,
1827. Doubtless the farm of Watchmanbrae, on the Eastern
face of the hill, was the residence of "the keipar of the fyir bitt"
thereon. The prospect from the summit is excellent, and the
sea horizon is about 36 miles distant. For a complete account of
this "miserable mountain", with the view therefrom, the reader
is referred to an article by Mr. Alexander Copland in "The
Cairngorm Club Journal" Vol. I. (1896). A few, however, of
the more noted points may be mentioned here : the Girdle
Ness Lighthouse, Loch of Loirston, the Blue Hill, Boswell's
Monument, Cairn-mon-earn, Kerloch, Clochnaben, Scolty,
Mount Battock, Mount Keen, Hill of Fare, Lochnagar,
Barmekin of Echt, Beinn a' Bhuird, Morven, Ben Avon, Hill
of Mortlich, Coillebhar, The Buck, Ben Rinnes, Tap o' Noth,
Bennachie, Hills of Foudland, Knock Hill, Hill of Mormond,

Collieston, Belhelvie Coastguard Station, the Bishop's Loch, Tarbathy, Donmouth and S. Machar Cathedral.

In 1515 the Town Council of Aberdeen resolved that the city marches should be gone round annually ; now intervals of twenty or thirty years are allowed to elapse, the last " Riding of the Marches" taking place on 4th September, 1889. The Doupin' Stane is near the middle of the round on Wineford, on the West side of Brimmond. It measures 12 feet by 10, and lies close to the 31st March Stone.

The parish of Newhills dates from 1666, previous to which it formed part of Old Machar. The first church of Newhills was built in 1662, at the expense of George Davidson of Pettens, Belhelvie ; it is now an ivy-clad ruin within the churchyard ; near by is the conspicuous modern building of 1830. Davidson richly endowed the new parish by a mortification of the lands of Kepplehills, which he had purchased from the town of Aberdeen, as a stipend for the minister. These lands, which are within the parish, extend to about 700 acres, and now yield a revenue much above the average stipend of the clergymen of the Church of Scotland. Near the church is a Convalescent Home, built in 1882 for the reception of poor persons in weak health who are likely to be benefited by change of air.

Auchmull is a name of considerable antiquity and still, in a restricted form, remains in use ; the Post Office spelled it Auchmill ; but the Railway Company called their station Buxburn, a corruption of Bucks-burn. There was a certain inconvenience in this arrangement and accordingly the parties interested recently agreed to use the name Bucksburn only. The Bucks Burn, which gives name to both village and station, rises at Rae-den (of old Roe-den) near Kingswells, on the East of Longcairn, and has a rapid course of about four miles to the Don. Up the pretty den forming the watercourse go the city children in search of the early primrose, the summer ferns and roses, the autumn rasps and brambles and hips and haws. The footpath on the wooded East bank is a favourite resort of all frequenters of the den. The rich meadow below, the black, rocky watercourse, and the steep, whin-covered banks on the West side are seen to advantage from the path. A pungent mineral well a few yards beyond Bucksburn House forms a natural termination to the walk.

Bucksburn.

The name Auchmull has been in use for over 500 years. The estate has undergone great changes, even since last century, as may be seen from the following extract from an advertisement dated 5th August, 1755 : " The Lands of Auchmull and Northfield, adjoining each other . . . have growing upon them above 500,000 trees of a considerable size, as Firs, Pines, Birch, Ash, Elm, Beech, Plane Tree, Allars, Hazel, Willows of all kinds, and some Oak and Limes, &c., with a breed of Deer, regular avenues, and a good prospect of the sea and adjacent country". The trees and the deer—where are they now? As for the fine mansion house—it latterly fell into the occupation of quarry workers!

The mills at the mouth of the Bucks Burn have had their vicisitudes; what was known as *the* Bucksburn Mills are now part of the large establishment of Mugiemoss Paper Works, belonging to Charles Davidson & Son, Limited. Charles Davidson, a millwright, started business at Mugiemoss in 1811, where he erected a Waulk Mill, a Flax-beating Mill, and, in 1817, a Snuff Mill. The Mills are now devoted to the manufacture of paper, and the business has increased to an enormous extent; the weekly output is over 120 tons, the workers numbering about 700.

Bankhead and Stoneywood are modern villages for the accommodation of the workmen at neighbouring mills and quarries. The Free and Episcopal churches are in Bucksburn; while at Bankhead is the church of the *quoad sacra* parish of Stoneywood, recently disjoined from Newhills. The road forks at Bucksburn; the North turnpike (on the left) proceeds by Craibstone and Tyrebagger, not coming into touch with the railway or the river till Kintore is reached; while (on the right) there is the Banff road. Meantime we follow the latter as far as the bridge over the Don at Dyce; thence the road on the left bank may be taken through New Machar and Fintray to Kintore. Leaving Bucksburn we pass through Bankhead (with Sclattie Quarry) and Stoneywood, the latter noted for its great paper works.

The Estate of Stoneywood, formerly called Craigharr, included at one time Waterton, Clinterty, and Greenburn. In

Stoneywood.

1373 part of Waterton was granted to Donald Bannerman, the King's physician; in 1454, Stoneywood became the property of the Frasers of Corntoun, near Stirling, who sold it in 1671 to John Moir of Kermuck, Ellon. The Moirs, who were strong Jacobites, held the estate till 1789, when it passed into the hands of James Forbes of Seaton, whose daughter and heiress married Lord James Hay. In 1877 James Gordon Hay sold to Alexander Pirie & Sons a large portion of Stoneywood, as well as parts of Auchmull and Sclattie, and also the lands of Mugiemoss and Bankhead, now known as the estate of Waterton. Paper-making was commenced at Stoneywood in 1770; now the works of Alexander Pirie and Sons, Limited (capital, £1,000,000), "are one of the greatest industrial establishments of modern times, most worthily representing, in every respect, the manufacture in which it is engaged. The works at Stoneywood are the largest of their kind in the United Kingdom, and send out their products to every part of the world". Woodside Works (see page 24) are used in conjunction with Stoneywood; also Union Works in Aberdeen for envelopes. The firm employs nearly 3000 workers.

According to Act of Parliament (1701) the proprietor of

Stoneywood had the right of holding "two yearly fairs at the Greenburn", but these markets have been discontinued since 1877, and the stance is now a cricket ground. The Sugar House marked on old maps is now represented by Bellfield Terrace.

Dyce is not a parish of great historic interest, and the situation of the railway station, built on the Muir of Dyce, did

Dyce.

did not at one time favourably impress the passing traveller. Gradually, however, the virtues of the Muir were recognised, and a village sprang up, which now enjoys an excellent suburban service. The principal estates, with their owners, in the parish, are :—Caskieben, James Stephen ; Kirkhill, Lady Carnegie ; Kinaldie, James Milne ; Parkhill, Testamentary Trustees of Alexander Gordon ; Pitmedden, George Thompson ; Woodlands, Trustees of Lord Sempill ; and Dyce Chemical Works, John Milne & Co., Limited.

The old parish church, with the churchyard, is within a bend of the Don, near the borders of New Machar and Fintray. At the East end of the church there are preserved two fine examples of the old sculptured stones of the district, which had previously been built into the wall of the churchyard. The new church has been placed nearer the centre of population, convenient for the village. According to tradition Dyce was at one time called the Chapel of S. Fergus, and was one of the six vicarages attached to the rectory of Kinkell. Between one and two miles west of the station is the farm of Standingstones on the Eastern slope of Tyrebagger Hill. Here, as the name implies, is a stone circle, a very complete example. The circle is nearly 60 feet in diameter, and consists of eleven upright stones and a big flat stone known as "the altar". The latter lies on the South side, and must have been brought from a distance, as it differs in quality from its fellows.

Pitmedden House is beautifully situated on the South side of railway, close to the station of that name. A little to the North-east a peculiar erection, standing in a field, attracts attention. It is a monument in memory of Dr. Duncan Liddel, a mathematician, who founded in 1613 several bursaries in Marischal College, from Pitmedden, of which he was then proprietor. There is also a cairn not without interest to Aberdonians ; it is situated on the highest point of the Pitmedden estate, and commands a fine view of the valley of the Don and of the North Sea. It is 16 feet in height, has a diameter of 18 feet at the base, tapering to 9 feet at the top. Built of solid masonry, it is ascended by a winding staircase, and surmounted by an iron railing with seats and flagstaff. On a slab of polished Corennie granite there are inscribed the family arms and the motto, "Per periculum vivo", and the following— "Erected on the fiftieth anniversary of Queen Victoria's first visit to Aberdeen, when she was received by George Thompson, Jr., Esq., then Lord Provost, and afterwards M.P. for Aberdeen".

The Buchan section of the Great North of Scotland Railway
leaves the main line at Dyce, and crossing the Don alongside
the road. enters the parish of New Machar.

New Machar. The principal estates with their owners, are :
Elrick and Swailend, Peter Burnet ; Goval
Bank, John Crombie ; Kingseat, Parish
Council of Aberdeen ; South Kinmundy, Rev. Duncan G.
Mearns ; Parkhill, Testamentary Trustees of Alexander Gordon ;
North Kinmundy, Mrs. Elizabeth Wilson and Trustees of the
late William Stephen ; Rainnieshill, William Watson ; and
Torryleith, Mrs. Irvine.

New Machar was part of Old Machar till 1521, and was
known as Upper Machar up to that date. In pre-Reformation
days it had been well supplied with places of worship—the
Church left little to be desired on that account ; the remains of
three may still be traced. The oldest, which dates previous to
1256, was S. Colms, at Monykebbuck : and there was a S.
Mary's both at Straloch and at Clubsgoval. The burial ground
in connection with S. Colms is still in use ; the chapel there
was deserted for the parish church in 1641. To the East of
Parkhill House there are three small lochs—Corby (mostly in
Old Machar), Lily and the Bishop's, the last formerly known
as Loch Goul. Corby Loch is the largest and the most uninteresting ; it is a "mere sheet of moss water, bordered with some
marsh plants, and stored with perch", and "well stocked with a
rare species of trout of excellent quality, averaging about half a
pound". Lily Loch is of small extent, and not unlike Corby
Loch in its surroundings. The Bishops of Aberdeen had,
before the Chanonry was built (and for some time afterwards),
their palace on an island in Loch Goul, some remains of which
still exist, and in summer, when the water is low, the site of the
buildings may be visited. In early times the loch had been of
much greater extent and surrounded by woodlands, the palace
having been connected with the mainland by a drawbridge.
Goval is the modern form of Goul, but the loch is now best
known as the Bishop's Loch.

"It looks liker a hermit's cell than a Bishop's palace, and
yet a great man lived and died there—I mean Bishop Benham"
[1279]. The islet had also a chapel in connection with the
Bishop's Palace.

Parkhill house is a spacious building, surrounded by fine
trees, with pleasure grounds fronting the Don for about a mile.
The original house was built by Skene of Lethenty, the place
being known before that time as Clubsgoval. Robert Gordon
of Straloch, the famous geographer, was born at North Kinmundy, in New Machar, in 1580. He was the first graduate
of Marischal College of Aberdeen, and is now best known from
his map of Scotland. His son, James, was the well-known
Parson of Rothiemay, while a grandson, Robert, was the
founder of Gordon's Hospital in Aberdeen.

Kingseat has been acquired by the Parish Council of

The Bishop's Loch

Aberdeen with the view of erecting an asylum for pauper lunatics.

Elrick Burn, known as Burn of Goval in its lower part, a tributary of the Don, divides the lower part of the parish. The old house of Rosehall, formerly called Boghall, stood about a mile North of the mouth of this burn between the road and the railway. At one time the patronage of New Machar was held by the proprietor of Rosehall "who did not scruple, when his presentee was objected to by both people and presbytery, to force him upon them, at the point of the sword, or more correctly by a 'riding committee', who, more quickly than Assemblies or Synods now-a-days, disposed of the doubts and objections of their rebellious flock and the recalcitrant presbytery". Rosehall now forms part of the estate of Parkhill.

The Donside road through Fintray leaves the Banff turnpike at Parkhill station. Passing through Goval (in New Machar) the traveller has, on the left, **Fintray.** Cothal Mills and Fintray House ; near the church is the village of Hatton of Fintray, close to the Don, of old crossed by a ferry ("Boat of Hatton") but now by a bridge. The latter is within a mile of Kinaldie station. But the left bank road may be continued to opposite Kintore, where there is also a bridge, or on to Inverurie through Keithhall. The principal estates, with their owners, in this parish are :—Fintray, Trustees of Lord Sempill ; Lairshill, Charles G. Stewart ; Wester Fintray and Balbithan, Earl of Kintore ; Disblair, Rev. Duncan G. Mearns ; Straloch, Mrs. Irvine ; and Dyce, William Philip.

Cothal Mills, near the New Machar boundary and opposite the old parish church of Dyce, were at one time leased by the present proprietors of Grandholm, but their importance now is very much decreased. There have been mills here for more than a hundred years. Immediately to the West is the site of S. Meddan's Church, with a grave-yard ; a building near by is still know as Old Manse. Fintray House, the principal mansion in the parish, overlooks the Don, and is conspicuous from the railway in the neighbourhood of Pitmedden station. It is built in the Tudor style and has finely wooded grounds. The lands of Fintray (along with Craigievar) were purchased in the beginning of the seventeenth century by William Forbes, a younger brother of Bishop Patrick Forbes of Corse, who acquired a large fortune as a merchant. His son, William, was the first Baronet of Craigievar. "The old name of Fintray House, or rather of the house which occupied the same site, was Lamington. The burgh of Inverurie once paid tithe to Lamington, a burden, indeed, from which, the writer is informed, they were only relieved about 1746 or 1747, by Sir Andrew Mitchell, who was about that time returned as M.P. for the burghs. There are those living who have heard old men tell of seeing the carts of Lamington come into Inverurie in harvest, and take away the tenth sheaf".—(Ramsay's "Guide to the Great

North of Scotland Railway", 1854). "This Craigievar road was titled from the tenantry of that estate carrying their victual rent by Kintore, crossing the Don there, on their way to Lamington (Fintray House), when it was a common saying among the good folks of Kintore, 'Gaither in your orra things, the honest men o' Craigievar's doon'".—(Watt's "Kintore", 1865).

Hatton of Fintray is rich ground for the antiquarian. Between the church and the river are the site of one of the Granges of the Abbey of Lindores, the remains of a Tolbooth, the supposed site of S. Giles's Chapel (with Graveyard) and Gallow Hill. A little to the North-east of the church is a supposed Mote Hill. The lands of Fintray belonged at one time to the Abbey of Lindores, and their house here was probably erected about 1386. James IV. spent a night here in his Northern Progress of 1497 ; the following extract is taken from the Lord High Treasurer's Accounts (Vol. I.) :—" Item, the third day of Januar, the king was in Fyntray, the abbot of Lindores place, giffin to Hannay, at the kingis command, to help to by him ane hors xxxj s ". Again in 1501 (Vol. II.) :— " Item, the xxvij day of October, in Fintray, to the preist that kepis the place, be the Kingis command xiiij s ". And in 1504 there is this entry also :—" Item, to the maister cuke he gaif to the preist of Fintree that kepis the place xiiij s ; Item, to him he gaif ane servand kepit the weschale thare iij s ". Nor was his Majesty then without diversion in his travels :—" Item, to the falconaris in Inverowry, the King being in Fyntree, to thair expens viij s ".

The following fragment was gleaned from tradition many years ago. It is named—

THE BONNIE LASS O' FINTRAY.

> I hae been in toun an country,
> I hae been 'mang far 'wa' gentry,
> But the bonny lass o' Fintray
>   She's the lassie I loe best.
>
>> Lassie wi' the yellow coatie,
>> Can ye lo'e a murlan Jockie ?
>> Lassie wi' the yellow coatie,
>> Think ye wad ye marry me ?
>
> O'er the muir an' throu' the boggie,
> Wi my lassie an' my doggie,
> Wha on earth could be sae happy
>   Wi a lass sae fair as thee ?
>
>> Lassie wi the yellow coatie, &c.

The haughs by the river side are much liable to floods, and have suffered severely in the great Don "spates". They are now protected as much as possible by embankments.

> Behold how Fintray's plains delight the eye.
> For fertile soil there's none with them can vie—
> See the enamelled meads extending wide
> Augment the river charms on every side.

This on the authority of "Don"; the plains still delight, and are more fertile than ever.

We now return to Bucksburn and resume our journey by the North road. Crossing Bucks Burn we are again reminded ot George Davidson's great liberality to the parish; the bridge here was built by him after, it is said, the drowning at the ford of several persons on the occasion of a great "spate".

Craibstone House will be passed on the left. The estate of Craibstone was bequeathed by Dr. Alexander Scott, a native

Craibstone.

of Huntly, for the erection and endowment of an Hospital in his native parish as a Home for the Aged. The Institution was opened in 1855. The grounds round Craibstone House contain some very fine specimens of trees— ash, elm, beech, plane, chestnut, silver fir and birch; larch and fir predominate in the plantations. A short distance beyond the house, close to the South side of the road, was the chapel of the Virgin Mary at Stoneywood, "at which there is a well resorted to in May"; the burial ground is still in use. The only vestiges of the building are a few of the foundation stones, turf covered, which are occasionally brought to view when a grave is dug. The size of the chapel appears to have been 30 feet by 17. Not very long ago there lived in a cottage hard by a woman who was famed for brewing ale and a good cup of tea. The popularity of her house was great till it was discovered that the liquid required in the production of these beverages was drawn from the centre of the churchyard. The road now climbs up Tyrebagger, and thence descends to Blackburn.

Tyrebagger Hill (823 feet) occupies the South-western portion of the parish of Dyce, and is divided from Brimmond

Tyrebagger Hill.

Hill by a hollow through which the road proceeds Westwards. The summit is crowned by the "Tappie", a stone and lime pile with a flight of steps, built in 1875 at the instance of Dr. William Henderson, then residing at Caskieben. The site was occupied by a cairn of loose stones. In the middle of the Tyrebagger woods, on the Hill of Elrick, is the so-called Robber's Cave, concerning which "The Statistical Account" (1793) says that "it is supposed by the vulgar (illiterate) to penetrate for miles underground, and celebrated in their legends as the residence of a noted robber and his gang. He was slain by an ancestor of the Johnstons of Caskieben, and the weapon employed on the occasion still makes a part of the arms belonging to that family. The cave is now shut up in order to prevent its harbouring foxes and other ravenous beasts". The old toll-house on Tyrebagger is at an altitude of 501 feet feet, while at Blackburn Bridge the height above sea level is only 245 feet. There are several quarries in this neighbourhood ; Clinterty will be passed on the right. Caskieben House—so named on the Johnstons ending their connection with the original Caskieben—overlooks on the right the little valley of Blackburn. The hamlet of Blackburn has a coach connection with Aberdeen, which is about eight miles distant. It is on the borders of Newhills, Dyce and Kinellar ; the nearest station for Blackburn and the Northern part of Kinellar is Kinaldie. A distillery was erected at Blackburn, but both it and the village which was to follow were failures.

The principal estates, with their owners in this parish are :—
Auchronie, Trustees of the late Dr. Thomas Farquhar ;
Cairntradlin and Kinellar, University of
Kinellar. Aberdeen ; Glasgoforest and Kinellar
Lodge, Mrs. Elphinstone Dalrymple ;
Kinaldie, James Milne ; and Tertowie,
James A. G. King

Kinellar Lodge is a modern building finely situated on a hill slope near the old mansion of Glasgoego. Tertowie House is on the South part of the parish, Kinaldie House in the North close to the railway station ; from which the church is about a mile South-west. The Muir of Kinellar, through which the road passes, was divided between the parishes of Kinellar and Kintore in 1840. As the burgh of Kintore is approached the road forks, the branch on the left leading direct, by Hallforest Castle, to Kemnay.

Look to Kintore, nor thou Eleusis shall,
Nor Sicily, thereafter fertile call.
Its fields are watered by the river Don,
Than which in Scotland pleasanter there's none ;
Herein are fishes in such plenty found,
That it may be called richer than the ground.

.   .   .

Here first I suck'd the Muses' breasts when young ;
It was here first I learned the Latin tongue.
Let Athens by Mæonian songs be raised ;
It's fit Kintore be by my verses praised.

THE present church of Kintore was built in 1819 on the site of the previous edifice, which is said to have been a facsimile of the church of Kinkell, and probably of the same date. Of that parish about one third, including Thainstone, was annexed to Kintore in 1754. Much of the burgh land, as well as the lands of Fintray, had probably belonged to the Abbey of Lindores ; the Free Church stands on Abbey ground. The town is built on both sides of the North road—an uncomfortable position as it found, to its cost, when armies marched through the burgh.

The Town House dates from 1737, and was then such an undertaking that it was not finished till 1747, even though it was erected at the charge at the Earl of Kintore. Previous to the latter date the Council generally met in the house of the presiding magistrate. The Town House, which was built on the market-stance, originally contained a Council room, a school-room and house, and a meal girnal, where the grain and meal of the Earl's tenants, who paid their rent in kind, were stored. Previous to the erection of the Town House, the bell was said to have been hung on a tree in the churchyard, not an unusual custom in the North. It is dated 1702, and bears the founder's name, Albert Gelly.

The burgh claims existence from the time of Kenneth II., but there is no trace of a charter, if it ever existed, to certify as to the date. Tradition opportunely steps in and thus accounts for the erection of the little Northern burgh : the good folks of Kintore had turned out to a man on a certain critical occasion, and, with their cattle covered with oak branches, made so formidable an appearance that the king gained a complete victory over his enemies. Thereupon he gave them the usual royal privileges over their lands and the wide moors and forest adjoining, and also fishing in the Don from Lady's Pot, upper end of Balbithan Island, to Pot Keello, near Kinaldie station.

An oak branch is prominent on the old seal of the burgh. In
later days the church claimed and exercised the exclusive
privilege of an acre of green sward for the cutting of turf to
cover graves in the churchyard. James IV., who several times
passed through Fintray, and possibly also Kintore, seems to
have been well disposed towards the Donside burgh, to which
he granted a charter in 1506.

James II. would appear to have been one of the monarc
who visited Kintore and Hallforest. Concerning his visit
tradition tells an interesting story, which is here given practically
in the words of Mr. William Smith, postmaster of Kintore,
1843 : " Sometime during the reign of James II. a person in the
garb of a traveller called one evening at a house in Kintore,
which appears to have stood on or near by the spot where the
Post Office now stands. The stranger, after discoursing a
while, and enquiring after the news of the place, asked the
goodman, whose name was Thain, if he knew anything about
the family of Hallforest Castle, and, on being answered in the
affirmative, he asked if Thain would carry a message from him
to Geordie Keith. 'Geordie Keith'! indignantly exclaimed
the goodman, 'a better man than you would have called him
Lord George Keith'. Thain, however, delivered his message
to Lord George Keith, who told him that the stranger was no
less a personage than the King. This information rather
staggered poor Thain, who was accompanied home by Lord
George. During his absence the goodwife suspected that her
visitor was more than he seemed, so she ordered the hen next
the cock to be dressed for his supper, and placed him in the
'bow' chair. For this piece of service my ancestor got a grant
of the piece of ground designated in the title deeds 'The Goose
Croft'. The family records from that time down to 1660 are so
decayed and dim that it seems to be impossible to read them ;
but at a Burgh Court on 16th August, 1661, we find that John
Smith, a burgess, inherited the ' Goose Croft', granted by the
King's majesty, as successor to his grandmother, Margaret
Thain. From the records that follow, it clearly appears that
this Margaret Thain was my great grandfather's great grandmother". The ' Goose Croft " lies between the road and the
railway, having the station at the North-west end. There are
other instances of long tenures in the burgh.

The chief magistrate of the burgh gave evidence before the
Royal Commissioners in 1833. There are several interesting
items in the report, from which the following particulars are
extracted. The census of 1831 shewed that the burgh had
86 houses, with a population of 402. It was then stated that it
possessed only a charter dated 1506 ; and all the town's lands
had been parted with between 1511 and 1609 to the Earls
Marischal, predecessors of the Earls of Kintore. The burgh
was then in the happy position of having neither property nor
debt ; its only revenne was a feu-duty of £9 4s. Scots, paid by
the Earl of Kintore, and £1 13s 4d. Sterling, paid annually by

the family of Craigievar to the poor of Kintore, as an amerce-
ment for the murder, within the burgh, of one of the family of
Gordon of Craigmyle. So little did the Provost then value the
dignity of his burgh that he expressed the idea that it "ought
to be relieved of the burdens incumbent upon a royal burgh,
and reunited with the county". The Commissioners in their
Report stated that Kintore was "in the most impoverished
condition of any town in Scotland".

One wonders if the shepherd of Kintore, whose office was
suppressed about ten years before, would have thus lightly
suggested the disappearance of the ancient burgh. He appears
to have been a person of some consequence, who put his spoon
into every brothpot in the town. We read that he had "a
salary of four shillings Scots for every kail yard or reeking lum
within the burgh, and three bolls two firlots of meal from Lord
Kintore for his portion of burgh lands. He had also a free
croft, and the privileges of any other burgher or inhabitant of
Kintore". About 1780, the sheep belonging to the burghers,
and pastured on the commonty, numbered between 1000 and
1500. But though the burgh dignitaries in 1833 suggested in
a very off-hand manner that an end should be made of their
independence, it would seem that a century previously the
rulers set some store on their rights. In 1736 the Earl of
Kintore was elected Provost, and "the whole liberties, privileges,
immunities belonging to an Burges and Gild brother were in
the most ample form given to The Right Hon. Mary, Countess
of Kintore", and two other ladies, while at the same time three
"servitours to the Right Hon. John, Earl of Kintore, were
made burgesses and Geld brethren gratis, in common and
ample form". In spite of the gloomy views of the Provost
and the equally gloom Report the little burgh remained a
distinct Corporation. When the railway was opened great
things were expected to happen : "crowds of visitors will come
out on holidays, and pleasure excursions will be frequent. The
capabilities of the place will be fully tested, and Mr. Gourlay of
the Kintore Arms will have enough to do to meet the demands
on his larder and his good humour. Moreover, as at Banchory,
feus will be in demand, and the merchant princes of Aberdeen
will be found erecting their villas by the side of the pretty Don".
Donside has profited much by the railway, but not Kintore in
any special manner ; "the merchant princes" have not come up
to expectations, but certainly the burgh now receives a fair
share of excursionists. It forms one of the group of "Elgin
burghs" in returning a Member to Parliament.

Arthur Johnston, of the ancient family of Caskieben
(Keithhall), the famous Latin poet, went to school at Kintore, as
he tells us in the lines at the head of this chapter. According
to him the burgh had formerly a race course, and in his time—
and later—pearls were found in the Don. As for the "fishes"
—the burgh water extends for nearly three miles on the right
bank of the river and is much "threshed" ; tickets may be

obtained from the burgh treasurer. The Don in this neighbourhood sometimes broadens to a lake in time of floods, notwithstanding its artificial embankments.

> Ye citizens o' auld Kintore,
> To whom the past is dear,
> Hae ye nae for the Castle Hill
> Ae tributary tear?

Kintore had at some remote time its castle, as is to be
inferred from its possession of a Castle Hill—till the railway
operations caused its removal. This conical mound stood
opposite the church, about 300 yards East from the station, and
was about 30 feet in height. Lately the Hill was one of the
commonties enjoyed by the burghers. The removal of the Hill
shewed that the upper ten feet had not formed part of the
original summit, and there were also indications that a building
of some sort had once on a time stood there. Edward I. passed
through Kintore in his march of 1296, and was at the "Manoir"
—which must have been Kintore Castle or Hallforest—on 20th
July.

The Council formerly took an intimate superintendence of
the affairs of the burghers. One cannot but admire the
shrewdness of the view taken in the following Minute concerning
those who endeavoured to dispense with a peat-stalk :—"Item,
it is statuted and ordained that whosoever indwaller in the
town shall be found not having pettis and kail yard after the
term, shall be reput as thieves, and put out of the town". The
burgh market, Marymass Fair, would seem to have been threatening collapse as far back as 1661, for then and later " The Court"
ordained the inhabitants "to compere personally" thereat with
their goods under the penalty of 3s. 4d. Scots. Insufficient
straw ropes and trespassing among "neighbours pease" were
offences dealt with by the "bailzie", who on the 6th July, 1694,
'statuted and ordained that whomsoever shall teadder yr beast,
with straw ropes, and shall not teadder their beasts sufficiently
shall pay 4s. Scots for ilk straw rope yt yr beast shall be tiddred
wt ; and ordains yt whomsoever shall be found amongst ye
neighbours pease, shall pay the sum of four pounds Scots, and
ye master to be comptable for his families, and lyable for ye
syme ". The latter clause may be called "paternal legislature",
but probably effected its purpose, as did the following :—"The
Bailzies statut and ordains that no person nor persons
within the burgh, shall resete any person or persons qr is
not honest, or is not able to provide him ym selves wt fyre, kail,
and other fwail, and if they do in ye contrary, the setter of the
house to be countable for all damages ye town or any person yr
from shall sustain ". Sheep-worrying dogs were as great a
trouble in those days as now, but in 1735 the Bailie was equal
to the occasion :—"The Bailie foresaid having considered the
above complaint, decerned and ordained the said William Rhind
to kill his dog immediately upon his going home, under failure

of £10 Scots money". There is nothing new under the sun ; even servants deserted their service in 1732 as in 1900, but the Barony of Kintore shewed such no mercy—the Bailie awarding as damages to the mistress the money part of the wages :—" The fee agreed on was eight marks (for the summer time), one pair of shoes or 7/o½ Scots, and one ell of linnen or two groats". Kintore had a noted witch, Issobell Cockie, but the local authorities sent her to Aberdeen to undergo her trial, which she did on 19th February, 1596, and was duly burned. Her " Dittay " is a most interesting document—too long, however, to be given here.

Hallforest Castle, about a mile to the South-west of Kintore, is one of the very few examples of the fourteenth century keeps now remaining in the North. The date of erection is uncertain, but Kennedy says that "according to tradition, it was built by King Robert Bruce for a hunting-hall. It consisted of four storeys, having embattlements, besides what is called a cape-house, with a movable ladder, by which those who occasionally lodged in it entered to the first floor. The Earl Marischal, having acquired a right to it from the Crown, presented it to his son, the first Earl of Kintore". The "New Statistical Account" says that it was "granted along with the surrounding domain, to Robert de Keith, Great Marischal of Scotland, after the battle of Inverurie, according to some, but according to others, after Bannockburn, in which he rendered essential service to the cause of Bruce". The castle is now a picturesque ruin, mainly a square block with two lofty arched apartments, the upper adorned with shrubs. In 1639 it was a residence of the Earl Marischal, and was subjected to several attacks during the wars of the Covenanters. A curious brass clock of the early years of the seventeenth century, removed from the castle, is now in Keith Hall. A few yards to the North-west of the Castle is the site of the Chapel of Hallforest.

Adjoining the burgh on the West is "Deer's Den" the supposed remains of a Roman camp. Until recently there were portions standing of the walls or dykes which had originally, it is computed, enclosed a space 800 by 500 yards. Between the road and the railway, as the town is entered from the South, is Tuach Hill (274 feet), almost surrounded by Tuach Burn on its crooked way to the Don. On this little eminence are Gallow Top, the remains of a stone circle, and a rock called the King's Seat. The Hangman's Croft—the occupant of which doubtless did duty on Tuach—was at the other end of the town, east of Bridgealehouse, which is on the West side of the road just before the Alford Valley Railway is crossed. In this neighbourhood is Campfolds, where Montrose encamped with 3000 men when on his way North in 1645. To the North-west is a large stone known as Cloven Stone, where Burgh Courts were sometimes held ; near by are Camie's Stone and Camie's Grave.

Thainstone House is opposite the fourteenth milestone, on the West side of the road. It is finely situated on Shaw Hill, among trees, about 320 feet about sea level, and commands an extensive view of the valley. There is a disused graveyard on the South side of the wood almost opposite the house. On the summit of Shaw Hill (572 feet), is Bruce's Camp where The Bruce lay previous to the battle of Inverurie. At Broomend, on the right bank of the Don, are the extensive paper mills of Thomas Tait & Sons—the reader is hereby presented with a specimen of their manufacture ; on the other side, almost opposite, is the ruined church of Kinkell. Between Thainstone and Port Elphinstone there are numerous Standing and Sculptured Stones as well as the remains of Stone Circles. Port Elphinstone, though in the parish of Kintore, is included within the parliamentary boundary of the burgh of Inverurie.

The principal proprietors in Kintore are the Earl of Kintore ; Trustee of the late John F. Mitchell (Thainstone) ; and Thomas Tait & Sons (Inverurie Mills).

In Watt's "Kintore" the author, after speaking of the antiquity of Bridgealehouse, goes on to say that "it is also associated with the old song of "The King and the Tinker", and he quotes stanzas from the ballad. Whatever tradition this statement may be based upon we know not ; but we do know that the locality of the ballad has been claimed for many places both in England and Scotland, from the latitude of Norwood in Surrey to Bridgealehouse, Kintore, with equal probability that it belongs to none of them. It is pure "Grub Street", and in all probability originated in the brain of some old Crowder who sang and hawked broadside ballads as a means of livelihood. For well nigh three hundred years there were no more popular ballads among the English peasantry than those which told of the chance meeting of the King (*incog.*) with some of his humbler subjects. Numerous samples have come down to us, from "John the Reeve", and "Rauf Coilyear" to "The King and the Forester", "The King and the Miller", "The King and the Tanner", "The King and the Shepherd", and "The King and the Farmer", "The King and the Hermit", in all their many varieties. "The King and the Tinkler" is a degraded version of a very common subject, and probably its best text is that which was taken down by J. H. Dixon from the singing of King "the Skipton Minstrel", and published in the Percy Society's "Poems, Ballads, and Songs of the Peasantry of England", (1846). Some local singer may have changed the line :—

"Till he came to an alehouse, hard by a woodside",

into :—

"Till he came to Bridgealehouse close to Donside".

and thus obtained the local association with Kintore.

> Thou art the town I love, which Ury's stream
> Doth water, and thou'rt calléd by its name.
> Don's crystal waters also flow to thee,
> Which, joined by Ury, much increased be.
>
> .   .   .   .   .
>
> Of thee if I do boast it is no shame ;
> In thee some special interest I claim—
> The land which fuel furnisheth to thee,
> It was the land of my nativity.
> Near thee it was I first drew vital breath ;
> I wish near thee, when old to meet my death.

INVERURIE, the prosperous capital of the Garioch, is a royal burgh near the confluence of the Ury with the Don. The town is mainly situated on the North road, the parlia· mentary boundary embracing Port Elphinstone, the old burgh, and the burgh muir— a length of about two miles. The extension of the town is provided for by side streets and branch roads, but the Inverurie of early times had probably been in the immediate vicinity of the confluence, hard by The Bass. There stood the church so recently as 1775, when a new and more conveniently situated edifice was erected, which latter was succeeded in 1842 by the present place of worship. The walls of the building left in 1775 were demolished about the beginning of the century, and the Kirkyard dykes built with the material.

The original burgh charter is not in existence, but was undoubtedly of anterior date to 1195 ; Queen Mary described Inverurie in 1558 as being then a burgh of great antiquity. The Bass was probably utilised as the first fortress of the little settlement, its position commanding the fords of the Don and the Ury. In Robertson's "Early Kings of Scotland" it is stated that in 878, on the succession of Aodh or Hugh, son of Kenneth Macalpine, first king of both Pictish kingdoms, his authority was disputed by Cyric, or Grig, a northern magnate. "Grig apparently invaded the immediate territories of Aodh, for in a contest in Strathallan, he was victorious, and Aodh, wounded and a prisoner, was conveyed to the fortress of Nrurin, where he died after a few weeks' captivity" ; Grig is said to have died at Dunnideer in 896. This is the first mention of Inverurie. Before 1176 the Castle of Inverurie was on The Bass, and was the principal seat of the royal Earldom of the Garioch. An old Scottish Act of Parliament appoints "the burgh of Inverauray to be the place where all Courts of Justice

and executions belonging to the regalitie of Garioch, as horn-
ings, inhibitions, etc., shall sit and be used ".

> The Dee and Don shall run in one,
> The Tweed shall run in Tay,
> And the bonnie water o' Ury
> Shall bear the Bass away.

Thus prophesied Thomas of Ercildoune, and " the inhabitants here ", says Sir James Balfour, " have this foolysche old
ryme always in their mouthes ".   The Bass is a truncated cone
of about forty feet in height with sides now so smooth that one
can almost understand why it was long regarded as artificial,
and that it covered the remains of " the plague " or something
equally mysterious.   But The Bass is alluvial, resting on a
bed of clay, and owes its existence solely to the two streams
which almost surround it, but which at one time had flowed at
a much higher level.   There is no lack of such mounds.   The
early inhabitants were shrewd enough to utilise such natural
advantages for defence ; other instances in Donside are the
Doune of Invernochty and the former Castle Hill of Kintore.
Adjoining The Bass on the East is a lower mound, oblong in
form, known as the Little Bass.   When the churchyard was
enlarged in 1883 both mounds were included within the fence,
and now form a picturesque feature of the ancient burial
ground.   The mingling of a portion of the Don's waters,
through the canal, with the Dee at Aberdeen Harbour mouth,
brought Thomas's rhyme again to notice, but The Bass is still
safe, though possibly not standing so " fast " as " Craigellachie ".

Bruce's camp was mentioned in the preceding chapter,
but the fight which ensued in 1308 is popularly known as the
battle of Inverurie, though fought at Barra in Bourtie.   " Bruce's
Cave " near by, on the South bank of the Don, opposite
Ardtannes, is suggestive as the hiding place of the king, who,
according to Barbour, lay sick in Inverurie on the eve of battle.
He, however, defeated the Comyns and pursued them into
Buchan.   The " cave " has disappeared, the steepness of the
percipitous bank there having probably caused a landslip.
There is another Inverurie battle to chronicle, but in much later
times, when Lord Lewis Gordon defeated the royalist troops in
1745 a little to the West of The Bass.

The ruins of S. Apolinarius's Chapel (colloquially Polnars
Chapel), surrounded by the ancient burial ground, are about two
miles Westward from The Bass on a picturesque knoll on the
North bank of the Don.   This saint was the patron of the
parish, and his name may be recognised in Polander Fair, as
one of the local markets was known.   The chapel, which had
measured about 36 feet by 18, is said to have been under the
church of Inverurie at The Bass ; but before its dedication to
S. Apolinarius (the first Bishop of Ravenna, ordained by the
Apostle Peter himself) it had probably been indebted for its
origin to the Culdees of Monymusk.   The place was originally

The Bass

called Rathael, and was part of the lands of Badifurrow, now Manar. It received the last name in 1808 from the new proprietor, who so called it from his former residence near the Straits of Manar, where he had acquired a fortune. Manar House is about a mile West from Polnar, and stands on the Southern face of a wooded hill overlooking the Don. Auch-orthies, about half a mile West of Manar House, was let upon a long lease in 1796 for founding the first Roman Catholic College in Scotland. The College was transferred to Blairs, in Mary-culter, in 1829, that estate having been bequeathed to the Catholics by the last Menzies of Pitfodels.

Port Elphinstone came into existence with the Canal, and was so named after Sir Robert Elphinstone the then baronet of Logie Elphinstone. Here the Don was laid under tribute, and supplied water to the Aberdeenshire Canal, and so the "Port" was a place of no small consequence. But when the railway made Inverurie its local head-quarters, its glory vanished, and its warehouses long remained empty. But the village main-tained an existence, and though it still lacks the bustle which distinguished it for nearly half a century, a fair amount of business is now transacted there. It is connected with Inverurie by a three-arched bridge, erected in 1791, over the Don at Coblehaugh.

Inverurie may be described as a little country town, an *Urbs in rure*, with all the adjuncts which modern demands require. It has long been a popular holiday resort for Aber-donians, and is favoured with a Saturday excursion train during the season. The railway company is removing the station to a more convenient point, and is also erecting large engineering locomotive works there—a removal from Kittybrewster—which must be of considerable benefit to the old burgh. The Don, as we have seen, is noted "for horn and corn", and Inverurie in particular, owing to its natural advantages, is largely interested in the cattle and grain trades. It is also a railway junction, a branch line (6 miles) leading to Oldmeldrum. The town has a spacious "market square", at the North end of which is the Town Hall. The inhabitants have the right of fishing on two good reaches, one on the Don and one on the Ury. The principal estates, with their owners, in the parish are : Ardtannes, Earl of Kintore ; Balquhain, Charles S. Leslie ; Braco, Francis R. Gregson ; and Manar, Henry Gordon.

We find that the authorities in Inverurie exercised as strict a surveillance over the citizens as did those in the neighbouring burgh. Thus on 1st June, 1605, the baillies, "with the consent of the hail community", restricted the number of "nowlt", "scheip", and "kow" to be kept by the burghers. Even the milking of the ewes had to be done to a general order of 9th June, 1607 : "all ewes within the toun to be milked at the buchts from this night furth". Nor were swine to be kept "except the owners keep them frae other men's skaith, either be corn, kell, or girs". Peas seem to have been as great a

temptation about three hundred years ago as suburban straw-
berry fields now are, say in Aberdeen. Kintore had to deal
with pea-stealers, and thus Inverurie "statut" on 11th August,
1618, "that the haill inhabitants be answerable ilk for his
familie, man, wyff, bairn, and servand, that nain gang to ony
man's peis, to pull or tak away any of thame". The drink trade
was also firmly handled, for on 18th March, 1608, not to mention
other individual cases : "it is statut and ordanit, in respect of
the informalitie of Ion Rae being so often mistemperit be drink,
that no browster give to the said John Rae nor sell him ony aill
within their hous, under pain of 40s., for ilk offence". On 4th
December, 1610, four men "are appoinit taisters tunsters of aill
within the bruch, whilk persons sall everie oulk ance visie the
taverners and their hous, and sett such prices on the aill as they
think the samyn worth on their consciences". In 1614 the
maximum price of ale was fixed at "12d the pynt", no measures
to be used except "sick as ar seilit with the commond seill of
the town". On 7th October, 1618, it was "Statute after this
day furth that na person within this bruch be extraordinar in
ther drynking, either be day or after nin hours at even". The
community boasted of a herd whose fee was thus fixed, "for
everie beast, except the hairst milk ky with their followers, ane
peck of meill, and everie auld sheep 12d., and for everie hog 6d.
But the ontaxmen to pay for their milk ky *pro rata*, because
they haiff no hainit girs of their own to keep their ky". The
herd's emoluments would appear to be rather irregula*r*, for three
years later the money fees are altered, and there is added "ane
cart full of peitts, of ilk househaulder who hav horse passing to
the moss ; and failing of the cartful of peitts sax shillings".
Thereafter a house seems to have been thrown in : "all
inhabitants who have hors, sall yok ane hors be sax hours on
the morning the 15th day of May, and bring in the lead faill
and divotts to the herds hous ; and also they that has not hors
to yok, to be thair thamselffs to big the said hous". In like
manner they had "to big and theik the mill" of Ardtannes. In
1615 the "haill indwalleris" were ordained to attend church
"before noon" and "efternoon" ; "na person outwith the aig of
fourteen yeirs be fund at the futball on the Sabothe days". The
same year the inhabitants were ordered to bring "hedder" to
thatch the kirk under a penalty of £10. In the year 1616 the
markets would appear to have been falling off, so all craftsmen
are ordered to bring their goods "upon everie Wednesday or
ordinarie market day" under a penalty of 40 shillings. In the
summer months the inhabitants were not allowed to "bring any
sheip to the hous, either to be milkit or otherwise, except to be
clippet, or to spain the lambis, but not to be kept or holdin fra
the fauld till the said lambis be fully spainit, but only to tak
them up, and the said lambis to be put out of the town and
spanit", all under a penalty of 40 shillings. Sheep-worrying
dogs were also a trouble, so on 7th March, 1617, an offender
was fined 33s. 4d. because he did not "put away his dog as a

schiep worrier". The following extract may fitly close these glimpses into burgh life in the Garioch in the early years of the seventeenth century : " 1629, 4th August. Alexander Fergus, *alias* Walace, in Inverurie, attached by the Sheriff of theft, and drowned in Ury, in the pot called the Ginken holl till he was deid ; buriet in the kirkyard of Inverurie".

> Beside the stream a castle proud
> Rises amid the passing cloud
>   And rules a wide domain
> (Unequal to its lord's desert).
> A village near with lowlier art
>   Is built upon the plain.
>
> Here was I born ; o'er all the land
> Around the Johnstons bear command,
>   Of high and ancient line ;
> Mantua acquired a noted name
> As Virgil's birthplace, I my fame
>   Inherit shall from mine.

The parish of Keithhall (anciently Montkeggie) is separated from Inverurie by the Don. Caskieben, the Latin poet's birth-place, has lost name, castle, and Johnstons ; **Keithhall.** it is now Keith Hall, the chief seat of the Earls of Kintore. Arthur Johnston was born here in 1587, and after some time passed at the Kintore school went to Marischal College, finishing his education abroad. He died in 1641. About 1662, Caskieben was purchased from the Johnstons by Sir John Keith. He was a son of the sixth Earl Marischal and was created first Earl of Kintore in 1667—in consequence of the share which it was *said* he took in the preservation of the Regalia of Scotland. Sir John Keith thereupon changed the name of the parish and of the house, which soon replaced that of the Johnstons. Keith Hall, which has been frequently altered and added to, is a large building in the Elizabethan style. The front is adorned with several family shields, the oldest of which is inscribed "E.I.K. : C.M.K. : 1665 : May . Truth . and . Grace . Rest . Here . In . Peace ". The house is situated on a broad plain on the East bank of the Ury, opposite the town of Inverurie, and has large and finely wooded grounds, which not only adorn the house, but from their vicinity add to the amenity of the ancient burgh. There are some remarkably fine old trees, including ash, elm, and plane. Part of the old mansion of Caskieben still forms a corner of the present house of Keith Hall, and near by is a green surrounded by trees, formerly a moat—another relic of the days when the Johnstons were proprietors. Externally, the mansion possesses little in the way of architectural adornment, the greyness of its hoary walls being relieved only by masses of ivy. But the surroundings are charming and picturesque. To the West is a flower garden, one of the chief adornments of which is a border of roses ; and in front the beautiful greens are intersected by a walk leading to a pond, used in the winter for skating and curling, beyond which the ground and shrubberies lead upward to the wooded heights beyond. The entrance hall is a very attractive apartment, with a low ceiling crossed by heavy oaken beams. The walls are of dark crimson, the floor is of red and yellow tiles, and at one end is a quaint fireplace. On the walls are arranged spears, arrows, etc., brought by the Countess from Australia. To the right as the visitor enters is the museum, full of rare and valuable curios from Japan and other foreign places visited by members of the family. An interesting historical relic, on the mantel-piece of the hall, is the key of Dunnottar Castle, which is preserved in memory of the first Earl of Kintore. A winding stair of stone, richly carpeted, leads to the upper floor, the walls of the staircase being also lined with spears. The drawing-room, a large, lofty apartment, is filled with family portraits, historic relics, and memories of foreign travel. Opening off the drawing-room is a Japanese sitting-room. An interesting discovery was made while recent alterations were going on. An old stone stair, leading from what was formerly the butler's room, was found inside the wall, at the side of the window. The steps, which are of stone and very narrow and steep, begin about three or four feet from the ground, and mount up, within the wall, to the older part of the house. The history of the stair is unknown, but it is evidently one of those secret stairs found in houses of the period, and intended for use in time of danger.

In the churchyard there was formerly a gravestone with this inscription : " Here lies John Boyle, wha ran with Lord Kintore mony a mile ". It seems that the Earl, who was not on the best of terms with his Countess, took rather a hasty farewell of her in Edinburgh on a certain occasion. As he mounted his horse he threw a shilling to John, and bade him make his way to Keith Hall as best he could—he himself was riding for life ! When the Earl reached Keith Hall he found his faithful servitor at the "loupin'-on-stane", ready to receive his horse.

Kinkell, or rather two-thirds of it, was united to Keithhall in 1754. Thus a parish of great antiquity, and which had originally six others under it, disappeared from modern history. Only its ruined church and a noted annual market keep its name before the public, though the official name of the conjoined parish is " Keithhall and Kinkell ". Kinkell probably signifies the head or principal church, for it was a parsonage, the subordinate parishes being Kintore, Kemnay, Montkeggie, Kinellar, Drumblade and Dyce. The ruined church probably dates from 1525, at which time the famous Alexander Galloway was parson, holding also office as a professor in King's College. The parson was a man who played many parts in his time. From the inscriptions still remaining it seems that the church was intended as a memorial to Galloway, and it was an elegant structure, measuring 80 feet by 24. According to tradition there was considerable treasure buried under the foundation

stone. A writer in 1732 thus describes the surroundings :—
" But this church is now so lamentably polluted and profaned
that one is ashamed to write of it". Jervise ("Epitaphs and
Inscriptions", Vol. I.) adds that this statement is applicable
"to the present state of the ruins, as well as to the burial-
ground". The ruin is still a "monument" worthy of preservation, and the attention of the heritors and the Ecclesiological
Society may fitly be directed to it. It contains a notable tombstone, enough of which remains to shew that it had covered the
remains of a knight, who, from the date (1411) thereon, had
probably fallen at the battle of Harlaw. This stone, which
covered one of the tombs of early date on which heraldic
cognisances are displayed, bears "two shields, one illegible,
the other with a chevron between two water budgets in chief
and a hunting horn in base, charges which are repeated on the
breast of the figure of a '*nobilis armiger*' carved on the stone,
believed to be Gilbert Greenlaw, who fell at Harlaw in 1411.
There is a Greek text from the New Testament on it, the
earliest instance, probably, in Scotland of such an inscription".—
(Sir John Balfour Paul's "Heraldry", 1900). Reverence for
antiquity and respect for the dead were not virtues in which
Kinkell excelled about three centuries ago, as this stone testifies.
For the reverse was utilised in 1592 to commemorate John
Forbes of Ardmardo ; the inscription is in Latin and the offence
therefore more heinous. It may be added that in 1771 the
church was unroofed to furnish materials for the new church of
the conjoined parishes—but that was only the custom of the
time. The baptismal font, which was the gift of Galloway, was
rescued from the ruins about the beginning of the century, and
is now in S. John's Episcopal Church, Aberdeen.

The principal estates, with their owners, in Keithhall, are—
Keithhall and Balbithan, Earl of Kintore ; Newplace, Synod of
Aberdeen ; and Kinmuck, University of Aberdeen. Balbithan
is an old mansion to the East of the church of Kinkell ; the
estate belonged to the Chalmers's from about the beginning of
the 16th century. The house stood formerly at Old Balbithan,
opposite Kintore ; but the laird is said to have removed because
a shot fired from Hallforest Castle reached his dwelling, and he
determined to go beyond the range of his "neighbour's" guns !
At the hamlet of Kinmuck—about half-way between the churches
of Fintray and Keithhall—is a small meeting house of the
Quakers, with a burial-ground.

> Gadie wi' its waters fleet,
> Ury wi' its murmur sweet,
> They hae trysted aye to meet
>   Amang the woods o' Logie.
> Like bride and bridegroom happy they,
> Wooing smiles frae bank and brae,
> Their wedded waters wind and play
>   Round leafy bowers at Logie.

The River Ury is the largest tributary of the Don, having a

length of 22 miles. Above Inverurie the valley of the Don,
with the exception of the alluvial basin
The Ury. forming the vale of Alford, is for the most
part, (we quote from "Memoirs of the
Geological Survey of Scotland",) narrow and
trench-like, while that of the Ury and its tributaries is broad in
proportion to the present volume of the stream. This fact,
together with the dominant course of the latter at Inverurie,
suggests the possibility that the course of the Don may have
been at one time to the North of Bennachie and the Correen
Hills, or at any rate that the Ury was once the more important
stream.

The Ury bears the simple name of the Glen Water in
the upper portion of its course.   It rises in Tod's Well,
Gartly, and flows through or along the following parishes,
Gartly, Drumblade, Insch, Forgue, Culsalmond, Oyne, Rayne,
Chapel of Garioch, Keithhall, Kinkell, and Inverurie.   Its
most noted tributary is the Gadie, concerning which, resist-
ing temptation, we simply refer the gentle reader to "Bennachie".

> Move noiseless, gentle Ury ! around my Jeannie's bed,
> And I'll love thee, gentle Ury, where'er my footsteps tread,
> For sooner shall thy fairy wave return from yonder sea,
> Than I forget yon lonely grave and all it hides from me.

So sang William Thom, "the Inverurie poet", who was
born in Aberdeen in 1798 or 1799.   His "Rhymes and Re-
collections of a Handloom Weaver" was published in 1844.
He died at Dundee on 29th February, 1848, and was interred
in the New Cemetery, where his tombstone is thus inscribed—
"To the memory of William Thom, the Inverurie Poet".   An
account of his life and poems is given in Walker's "Bards of
Bonaccord" (1887).

> West of Inverurie, about a mile or twa,
> On a bonny hill-head lies the town of Harlaw.

> .   .   .   .   .

> July the twenty-fourth, S. James's even,
> Harlaw was fought, fourteen hundred and eleven.

The Battle of Harlaw was fought in the neighbouring
parish of Chapel of Garioch.   The ballads, with notes, tell its
story at sufficient length for these pages.   It may, however, be
added that the Mill of Maryculter Friendly Society (see
"Deeside", 3rd Ed. p. 44), visited the field on 24th July, 1841,
the anniversary of the battle.   Their chairman on that occasion
was Mr. Thomas Blaikie, Lord Provost of Aberdeen, an
appropriate selection, seeing that the reputed armour of the
Aberdeen Provost who fell at Harlaw stands in the vestibule of
the Town Hall.

THE BATTLE OF HARLAW.

Foughten upon Friday, July 24, 1411, against Donald of the Isles.

Frae *Dunideir* as I cam throuch,
 Doun by the Hill of *Banochie,*
Alangst the Lands of *Garioch ;*
 Grit Pitie was to heir and se
 The Nays and dulesum Hermonie,
That evir that dreiry Day did daw,
 Cryand the *Corynoch* on hie,
Alas ! Alas ! for the *Harlaw.*

I marvlit quhat the Matter meint,
 All Folks war in a fiery fairy :
I wist nocht quha was Fae or Freind ;
 Zit quietly I did me carrie.
 But sen the Days of auld King *Hairy,*
Sic Slauchter was not hard nor sene,
 And thair I had nae Tyme to tairy,
For Bissiness in *Aberdene.*

Thus as I walkit on the Way,
 To *Inverury* as I went,
I met a Man and bad him stay,
 Requeisting him to mak me quaint,
 Of the Beginning and the Event,
That happenit thair at the *Harlaw ;*
 Then he entreited me tak tent,
And he the Truth sould to me schaw.

Grit *Donald* of the *Yles* did claim,
 Unto the Lands of *Ross* sum Richt,
And to the *Governour* he came,
 Them for to haif gif that he micht :
 Quha saw his Interest was but slicht ;
And thairfore answerit with Disdain ;
 He hastit hame baith Day and Nicht,
And sent nae Bodward back again.

But *Donald* richt impatient
 Of that Answer Duke *Robert* gaif,
He vowd to GOD Omnipotent,
 All the hale Lands of *Ross* to haif,
 Or ells be graithed in his Graif.
He wald not quat his Richt for Nocht.
 Nor be abusit lyk a Slaif,
That Bargain sould be dearly bocht.

Then haistylie he did command,
 That all his Weir-Men should convene,
Ilk an well harnisit frae Hand,
 To meit and heir quhat he did mein ;
 He waxit wrath and vowit Tein,
Sweirand he wald surpryse the Forth,
 Subdew the Burgh of *Aberdeen,*
Mearns, Angus and all *Fyfe,* to *Forth.*

Thus with the Weir-men of the *Yles*,
　　Quha war ay at his bidding bown,
With Money maid, with Forss and Wyls,
　　Richt far and neir baith up and doun :
　　Throw Mount and Muir, frae Town to Town,
Alangst the Land of Ross he roars,
　　And all obey'd at his Bandown,
Evin frae the *North* to *Suthren* Shoars.

Then all the Countrie Men dld zield ;
　　For nae Resistans durst they mak,
Nor offer Battill in the Feild,
　　Be forss of Arms to beir him bak ;
　　Syne they resolvit all and spak,
That best it was for their Behoif,
　　They sould him for their Chiftain tak,
Believing well they did him luve.

Then he a Proclamation maid
　　All Men to meet at *Inverness*,
Throw *Murray* Land to mak a Raid,
　　Frae *Arthursyre* unto *Spey-ness.*
　　And further mair, he sent Express,
To schaw his Collours and Ensenzie,
　　To all and sindry, mair and less,
Throchout the Boundis of *Boyn* and *Engie.*

And then throw fair *Strathbogie* Land,
　　His Purpose was for to pursew,
And quhasoevir durst gainstand,
　　That Race they should full sairly rew.
　　Then he bad all his Men be trew,
And him defend by Forss and Slight,
　　And promist them Rewardis anew,
And mak them Men of mekle Micht.

Without Resistans as he said,
　　Throw all these Parts he stoutly past,
Quhair sum war wae, and sum war glaid,
　　But *Garioch* was all agast.
　　Throw all these Feilds he sped him fast,
For sic a Sicht was never sene ;
　　And then, forsuith, he langd at last
To se the Bruch of *Aberdene.*

To hinder this prowd Enterprise,
　　The stout and michty Erle of MARR
With all his Men in Arms did ryse,
　　Even frae *Curgarf* to *Craigyvar*,
　　And down the syde of *Don* richt far,
Angus and *Mearns* did all convene
　　To fecht, or DONALD cam sae nar
The Ryall Bruch of *Aberdene.*

And thus the Martial Erle of MARR,
   Marcht with his men in richt Array,
Befoir the Enemie was aware,
   His Banner bauldly did display.
   For well enewch they kend the Way,
And all their Semblance weil they saw,
   Without all Dangir, or Delay,
Came haistily to the HARLAW.

With him the braif Lord OGILVY,
   Of *Angus* Sherriff principall,
The Constabill of gude *Dunde*,
   The Vanguard led before them all.
   Suppose in Number they war small,
Thay first richt bauldie did persew,
   And maid their Faes befoir them fall,
Quha then that Race did sairly rew.

And then the worthy Lord SALTON,
   The strong undoubted Laird of DRUM,
The stalwart Laird of *Lawristone*,
   With ilk thair Forces all and sum.
   PANMUIR with all his Men did cum,
The Provost of braif *Aberdene*,
   With trumpets and with Tuck of Drum,
Came schortly in thair Armour schene.

These with the Erle of MARR came on,
   In the Reir-ward richt orderlie,
Thair Enemies to sett upon ;
   In awful Manner hardily,
   Togither vowit to live or die,
Since they had marchit mony Mylis
   For to suppress the Tyrannie
Of douted DONALD of the *Yles*.

But he in Number Ten to Ane,
   Richt subtilie alang did ryde,
With *Malcomtosch* and fell *Maclean*,
   With all thair Power at thair Syde,
   Presumeand on thair Strenth and Pryde,
Without all Feir or ony Aw,
   Richt bauldlie Battill did abyde,
Hard by the Town of fair HARLAW.

The Armies met, the Trumpet sounds,
   The dandring Drums alloud did touk,
Baith Armies byding on the Bounds,
   Till ane of them the Feild sould bruik.
   Nae Help was thairfor, nane wald jouk,
Ferss was the Fecht on ilka Syde,
   And on the Ground lay mony a Bouk.
Of them that thair did Battill byd.

With doutsum Victorie they dealt,
  The bludy Battil lastit lang,
Each Man his Nibours Forss thair felt ;
  The weakest aft-tymes gat the Wrang :
  Thair was nae Mowis thair them amang,
Naithing was hard but heavy Knocks,
  That Eccho made a dulefull Sang,
Thairto resounding frae the Rocks.

But *Donald's* Men at last gaif back ;
  For they were all out of Array.
The Erle of MARRIS Men throw them brak,
  Pursewing shairply in thair Way,
  Thair Enemys to tak or slay,
Be Dynt of Forss to gar them yield,
  Quha war richt blyth to win away,
And sae for Feirdness tint the Feild.

Then *Donald* fled, and that full fast
  To Mountains hich for all his Micht ;
For he and his war all agast,
  And ran till they war out of Sicht :
  And sae of *Ross* he lost his Richt,
Thocht mony Men with him he brocht,
  Towards the *Yles* fled Day and Night,
And all he wan was deirlie bocht.

This is, (quod he) the richt Report,
  Of all that I did heir and knaw,
Thocht my Discourse be sumthing schort,
  Tak this to be a richt suthe Saw ;
  Contrairie God and the King's Law,
Thair was spilt mekle Christian Blude,
  Into the Battil of *Harlaw* ;
This is the Sum, sae I conclude.

But zit a bony Quhyle abyde,
  And I sall mak thee cleirly ken
Quhat Slachter was on ilkay Syde,
  Of *Lowland* and of *Highland* Men,
  Quha for thair awin haif evir bene :
These lazie Lowns micht weil be spaird,
  Chessit lyke Deirs into thair Dens,
And gat thair Waiges for Rewaird.

MALCOMTOSH of the Clan Heid Cheif,
  Macklean with his grit hauchty Heid,
With all thair Succour and Releif,
  War dulefully dung to the Deid ;
  And now we are freid of thair Feid,
They will not lang to cum again ;
  Thousands with them without Remeid,
On *Donald's* Syde that Day war slain.

And on the uther Syde war lost,
  Into the Feild that dismal Day,
Chief Men of Worth (of mekle Cost)
  To be lamentit sair for ay.
  The Lord *Saltoun* of *Rothemay*,
A Man of Micht and mekle Main ;
  Grit Dolour was for his Decay,
That sae unhappylie was slain.

Of the best Men amang them was,
  The gracious gude Lord OGILVY,
The Sheriff-Principal of *Angus*,
  Renownit for Truth and Equitie ;
  For Faith and Magnanimitie ;
He had few Fallows in the Field,
  Zit fell by fatall Destinie,
For he nae ways wad grant to zield.

Sir *James Scrimgeor* of *Duddap*, Knicht,
  Grit Constabill of fair *Dunde*,
Unto the dulefull Deith was dicht,
  The King's cheif Banner-man was he,
  A valziant Man of Chevalrie,
Quhais Predecessors wan that Place
  At *Spey*, with gude King WILLIAM frie,
Gainst *Murray* and *Macduncan's* Race.

Gude Sir *Alexander Irving*,
  The much renownit Laird of *Drum*,
Nane in his Days was bettir sene,
  Quhen they war semblit all and sum ;
  To praise him we sould not be dumm,
For Valour, Witt and Worthyness,
  To End his Days he ther did cum,
Quhois Ransom is remeidyless.

And thair the Knicht of *Lawriston*
  Was slain into his Armour schene,
And gude Sir *Robert Davidson*,
  Quha Provest was of *Aberdene*,
  The Knicht of *Panmure*, as was sene,
A mortall Man in Armour bricht,
  Sir *Thomas Murray* stout and kene,
Left to the Warld thair last gude Nicht.

Thair was not sen King *Keneths* Days
  Sic strange intestine crewel Stryf
In *Scotland* sene, as ilk Man says,
  Quhair mony liklie lost thair Lyfe ;
  Quhilk maid Divorce twene Man and Wyfe,
And mony Childrene fatherless,
  Quhilk in this Realme has bene full ryfe ;
LORD help these Lands, our Wrangs redress.

In *July*, on Saint *James* his Even,
    That Four and twenty dismall Day,
Twelve hundred, ten Score and eleven
    Of Zeirs sen CHRYST, the Suthe to say :
Men will remember as they may,
    Quhen thus the Veritie they knaw,
And mony a ane may murn for ay,
    The brim Battil of the *Harlaw.**

*From Ramsay's " Evergreen," 1724. The exact age of the poem (for it is not in the ordinary or popular ballad style) has never been ascertained. Ritson, Pinkerton, and others maintain that judging from its manner, it might have been written soon after the event :—while Lord Hailes, and Sibbald (" Chronicle of Scottish Poetry," III. p. 288.) believed it to be of the days of Queen Mary, or James VI. Its name is mentioned in " The Complaint of Scotland," 1549, as one of the popular songs of the period. Ramsay is supposed to have printed it from some broadside copy—and may probably have touched it up as he did most of the old poems and songs which passed through his hands. The late Mr. Norval Clyne pointed out that the author had used Boece's History, and altogether the best authorities now accept Lord Hailes' judgment and look on the ballad, *as we now have it,* as a product of the same period which gave us two others, with strong family likeness, " The Battle of Balrinnes " (1595) and " The Raid of the Reid-Swyre " (1575).—We know of no better account of the battle than it contains.

THE BATTLE OF HARLAW.

1. As I cam in by Dunidier,
    An doun by Netherha,
There was fifty thousand Hielanmen
    A-marching to Harlaw.
      Wi a dree dree dradie drumtie dree.

2. As I cam on, an farther on,
    An doun an by Balquhain,
Oh there I met Sir James the Rose,
    Wi him Sir John the Gryme.

3. ' O cam ye frae the Hielans, man ?
    An cam ye a' the wey ?
Saw ye Macdonell an his men,
    As they cam frae th= Skee ? '

4. ' Yes, me cam frae ta Hielens, man,
    An me cam a' ta wey,
An she saw Macdonel an his men,
    As they cam frae ta Skee.'

5. ' Oh was ye near Macdonell's men ?
    Did ye their numbers see ?
Come, tell to me, John Hielanman,
    What micht their numbers be ? '

6. ' Yes, me was near, an near eneuch,
    An me their numbers saw ;
There was fifty thousan Hielanmen,
    A-marchin to Harlaw.'

7. 'Gin that be true,' says James the Rose,
   , We'll no come meikle speed ;
  We'll cry upon our merry men,
    And lichtly mount our steed.'

8. 'Oh no, oh no,' says John the Gryme,
   'That thing maun never be ;
  The gallant Grymes were never bate,
    We'll try phat we can dee.'

9. As I cam on, an farther on,
   An doun an by Harlaw,
  They fell fu close on ilka side,
    Sic fun ye never saw.

10. They fell fu close on ilka side,
   Sic fun ye never saw ;
  For Hielan swords gied clash for clash
    At the battle o Harlaw.

11. The Hielanmen, wi their lang swords,
   They laid on us fu sair,
  An they drave back our merry men,
    Three acres breadth and mair.

12. Brave Forbes to his brither did say,
   Noo brither, dinna ye see?
  They beat us back on ilka side,
    An we'se be forced to flee.

13. 'Oh no, oh no, my brither dear,
   That thing maun never be ;
  Tak ye your good sword in your hand,
    An come your wa's wi me.'

14. 'Oh no, oh no, my brither dear,
   The clans they are ower strang,
  An they drive back our merry men,
    Wi swords baith sharp an lang.'

15. Brave Forbes drew his men aside,
   Said, Tak your rest a while,
  Until I to Drumminor send,
    To fess my coat o mail.

16. The servan he did ride,
   An his horse it did na fail,
  For in twa hours an a quarter
    He brocht the coat o mail.

17. Then back to back the brithers twa
   Gaed in amo the thrang,
  An they hewed doun the Hielanmen,
    Wi swords baith sharp and lang.

18. Macdonell, he was young and stout,
    Had on his coat o' mail,
An he has gane out throw them a',
    To try his han himsell.

19. The first ae straik that Forbes strack,
    He garrt Macdonell reel,
An the neist ae straik that Forbes strack,
    The great Macdonell fell.

20. An siccan a lierachie
    I'm sure ye never saw
As was amo the Hielanmen,
    When they saw Macdonell fa.

21. An whan they saw that he was deid,
    They turned an ran awa,
An they buried him in Leggett's Den,
    A large mile frae Harlaw.

22. They rade, they ran, and some did gang,
    They were o sma record ;
But Forbes and his merry men,
    They slew them a' the road.

23. On Monanday, at mornin,
    The battle it began,
On Saturday, at gloamin,
    Ye'd scarce kent wha had wan.

24. An sic a weary buryin
    I'm sure ye never saw
An wis the Sunday after that,
    On the muirs aneath Harlaw.

25 Gin ony body speer at you
    For them ye took awa,
Ye may tell their wives and bairnies
    They're sleepin at Harlaw.*

*Communicated to Professor Child " by C. E. Dalrymple, Esq. of Kinaldie, Aberdeenshire, in 1888, as obtained from the country people by himself and his brother, fifty years before." It was first printed by Professor Aytoun in his "Ballads of Scotland," 2 vols., 1858, with some editorial changes. Another version appeared in "Notes and Queries," and was incorporated in Maidment's "Scottish Ballads and Songs," 2 vols., 1868; but both Aytoun's and Maidment's are founded on a copy of Mr. Dalrymple's text. We give this version, disfigured and distorted almost to burlesque as it is, as a supplement to the older poem, because, though by no means an ancient ballad, it is truly traditionary, and has been sung by the peasantry of the district for many generations. From its total want of reference to the Earl of Mar, and the many other men of great local distinction who took part in the battle, Professor Child is disposed "to believe that this particular ballad had its rise in comparatively recent times;" and we expect few, acquainted with ballad lore, will dissent from that finding. Indeed the introduction of a Rose (mistaken by the singer for "Sir James" of ballad fame) and the prominence given to the prowess of Forbes— seem to have been caught from some crude tradition of the account of the battle given in "Don, a Poem," 1742.

VI.—INVERURIE TO ALFORD

Bloodthirsty Dee,
Each year needs three ;
But bonny Don,
She needs none.

THIS section of our journey contains some of the most picturesque scenery to be found in the Don valley. There are two roads along the river, one on each bank ; that on the left leaves the North road close to Inverurie Bridge, and the other at no great distance South in the village of Port Elphinstone. The former passes through the parishes of Inverurie, Chapel of Garioch, Monymusk, Oyne, Keig, and Tullynessle-Forbes ; the latter Kintore, Kemnay, Monymusk, Tough and Alford. The stations on the Alford Valley Railway are :—

Miles.		Miles.	
(from Aberdeen.)		(from Aberdeen.)	
13¼	Kintore.	24	Tillyfourie.
17¾	Kemnay.	26¼	Whitehouse.
23¾	Monymusk.	29¼	Alford.

Kemnay station is also conveniently situated for Blairdaff and the South part of Chapel of Garioch ; Monymusk and Tillyfourie for Cluny ; Tillyfourie also serves part of Tough ; and Whitehouse for Keig and Tough. The railway approaches the river on the North side of Kemnay Paradise quarries, and is at its greatest distance at Tillyfourie, having the Menaway range between that station and the Don.

Leaving Kintore by rail nothing particularly attracts attention till Paradise Hill is neared. Here are the celebrated Kemnay granite quarries : "it is a fine-grained, compact, light grey, or nearly white rock, composed of white plagioclase, microline, quartz, and two micas. Large quarries have been opened in this rock at Kemnay and Tomsforest, besides many other smaller workings ; and at the former locality the granite has been largely wrought" since 1858, when it was leased by Mr. John Fyfe. The Paradise quarry was, however, opened in 1830 by Mr. John Burnett of Kemnay, in connection with extensive additions and alterations to Kemnay House. In the Kemnay quarries the white rock is accompanied by bands of a coarser pinkish variety, while both are traversed by thin vertical and oblique dykes of grey mica-trap. These quarries give employment to about 400 men, and are splendidly equipped with all the latest appliances for carrying on the work most effectively and expeditiously. Sometimes a block as large

Kemnay.

as thirty feet long, and weighing over a hundred tons, has been dispatched for the service of the builder. The Holborn Viaduct in London, with the exception of the red part, which came from Mull, but which was brought to Kemnay to be dressed, was built from the Kemnay quarries, as was also the Thames Embankment and the Forth Bridge. Another quarry, called Leshangie, at the Southern extremity of the parish, contains granite of a still finer quality than the others. The Porter's Lodge, at the extremity of the West Avenue to Kemnay House, close by the proprietor's chapel, is built of this stone, and is much admired, being considered the most beautiful Lodge in this part of the country. Another quarry at Whitestones, on the East side of Lochshangie Hill (547 feet), has, till recently, been much worked for the last hundred years. A great part of Waterloo Bridge, London, as also New London Bridge, were built out of it. Some think it the best Kemnay granite, and had another route, on the South side of the parish, been followed for the Alford Valley Railway, it would have brought better stone into the market, from both this and the Leshangie quarry. This somewhat nearer line would also have saved a very awkward curve in Tom's Forest, which always demands care and reduction of speed with the trains. The remains of other quarries exist on Lochshangie Hill, which have been worked at remoter periods. This hill commands a fine view of Kintore and neighbourhood, with Hallforest Castle.

The village of Kemnay, clustered about the station, owed its birth to the railway ; it has recently much increased in size, partly on account of the neighbouring quarries. In 1831 the population was only 616 ; it is now nearly 3000—a phenomenal increase for the North of Scotland. Even when the present proprietor succeeded, there were more beasts than people, and not one slated dwelling house except his own and the Manse. When, after the destruction of the old thatched mill-house by the flood of 1829, a new slated house was erected, it was looked upon as a daring innovation. The village owes not a little to the amenity of its situation ; there is no lack of wood, and near by is the Don, on which is a bridge leading across to Blairdaff. Bennachie gives character also to the neighbourhood, and altogether the prosperity and popularity of Kemnay need not be wondered at. The village has now an excellent water supply, which cost the ratepayers £4000, and it rejoices also in a chalybeate spring, which, according to "Don", is "nothing inferior to Pannanich". This spring, near the farm of Milltown, was analysed by the late Dr. Marsack of Tunbridge Wells, who pronounced it, for a certain class of patients, superior to the famed Tunbridge Wells waters ; and was even prepared to send such patients to Kemnay. In the course of improvements on the farm, a ditch near by this spring was deepened to such an extent that a later analysis, by the same celebrated chemist, disclosed the fact that it then remained only a good chalybeate, the other ingredients being gone. Thus a possible source of profit to Kemnay became lost, but the proprietor proposes to collect the now amissing parts of the original well.

Bennachie must needs come often into these pages; it is thus referred to by an Aberdeen poet :—

> O, the woods were green as ever,
>   And the wimpling of the river
> Was pleasant—as it aye was at Kemnay ;
>   And the sunset bonnilie,
>   Frae the back o' Bennachie
> Sent a glowin' smile to me at Kemnay.

> Ah, me ! it's strange, it's strange !
>   But that rugged mountain range
> That you see against the glowin' sky at Kemnay—
>   I am now a grey-haired carle,
>   And have wandered thro' the warl',
> But seen naething like a sunset from Kemnay.

The Lang Stane o' Craigearn is a noted monolith and, standing on high ground, is a sort of landmark ; it is about 12 feet in height. Another stone, within the wood on Parkhill, which is seen from the parish church, was, according to a modern ballad, thrown from Bennachie by the Devil at the priest of Kemnay :—

> But the fervent prayers o' the holy priest,
>   And the power o' the sweet Sanct Anne,
> They turned the murderous rock aside,
>   And foiled the foul fiend's plan.
> And it lichted doon frae the darkened lift,
>   Like the greedy erne bird,
> And there it sits in the Kirk-lands yet,
>   Half buried in the yird.

There are about a dozen such enormous stones within a small radius, most probably glacier-borne from the Cairngorms ; one is known as the " Grey Stone ".

The destruction of the old parish church—to make room for a new building—in 1844, is now much deplored. The high altar was beautifully apparent, though it had been built over at the Reformation. A new site should have been provided, and the ancient building maintained as a relic ; the belfry, however, which only dates from 1632, is preserved in the proprietor's flower garden.

From several coigns of vantage in the immediate vicinity of the village splendid views of the surrounding country—the tortuous course of the wimpling Don, the richly-wooded patches, the undulating pastoral fields, and the heights of Bennachie, Cairn William, and Pitfichie in the background—can be gained ; but perhaps the finest prospect of all can be secured by taking one's stand at the doorway of the Free Church. A more extended view of the parish may be had from the top of Paradise Hill which seems to have derived its name from the view. Till very recently many salmon were caught in the cruives belonging to the miller, but through neglect the right has been lost".

The estate of Kemnay (Alexander G. Burnett) comprises about fifteen-sixteenths of the parish, the other sixteenth being held by the Earl of Kintore and Mrs. Mackenzie-Fraser of Castle Fraser. The Burnetts have held Kemnay since 1688, when Thomas Burnett purchased it from Sir George Nicolson, Lord Kemnay. His son, also Thomas Burnett, a man of some distinction and sterling worth, being a literary character, was the friend of Leibintz, whose letters to him are preserved at Kemnay House. Though a most inoffensive individual, in consequence of a political pamphlet which he published while in Paris, he was seized and imprisoned in the Bastile, where he was subjected to such tortures as would have ended his life, had he not been set at liberty through the intercession of one of the ladies of the French Royal household. He was the first Burnett who lived at Kemnay. When he came to it, after these troubles, he found the house a small castelated building on a sand hillock, in peat moss, facing Bennachie. In the year 1770 he planted, on another hillock on the moss, a double row of beeches which was called the Green Avenue. A small part of it, that next the House, was cut as a hedge, but his son, when he succeeded, would not allow a knife to touch it, and from that time the trees grew up, though they have never had the same appearance as the others. The father of the present proprietor, however, on the making of the Alford turnpike, induced the Road Trustees to take the road round through the peat moss, it having previously passed the Northern end of the hillock, at the termination of the Green Avenue, on which was a clump of Beeches, it being precipitous down to the road, the whole of the peat moss being soon after trenched and drained. It may be noted that the third proprietor of Kemnay was the first recorded Provost of Inverurie, the chief magistrate, until his time, having been designated Baillie. The fourth proprietor was Alexander Burnett, who, from 1756 to 1778, was Secretary of Embassy at the Prussian Court, and, for a short time afterwards, Chargé d' Affaires. He gained considerable reputation, and was very much trusted by Frederick the Great, a picture of whom (among other old and valuable paintings) adorns the walls of Kemnay House.

The old house of Kemnay is stated to date from the end of the fifteenth century. There is, however, none of the original building now remaining, with the exception of vaulted cellars, a fine old spiral staircase, and a turret with small room attached. When George Burnett, the first Provost of Inverurie, took up his residence there, the surroundings were bleak and cheerless. Before he died the pleasure grounds of Kemnay had the reputation of being the most beautiful in Scotland. The "Wilderness", as the ground here was formerly suitably named, became an ornamental plantation of choice trees, with a labyrinth of grass walks, a pond, and a "hermitage", all laid out in

Kemnay House

conformity with the quaint fashion of the day, making it the show place of the district. A subsequent proprietor, however, allowed the formal parterres and flower gardens in the Italian style to fall into neglect, and the improvements since effected have greatly altered their character. The Beech Avenue leads from the railway station, and terminates near a sweep of lawn in front of the house. This avenue is, though no longer green, still unsurpassed in Scotland, and equalled perhaps only by that at Inverary Castle ; these two-century old giants overarch, and in the summer time form an aisle of greenery. The spiral staircase is said to be the oldest in Aberdeenshire ; the steps, which are of granite and not equi-distant, certainly bear the stamp of age. No country mansion would be complete without its haunted chamber ; in this instance the turret room serves. The story goes that one Morrison, who was factor on the estate before the Burnetts purchased it, was the chief actor in a murder committed in the room in which he afterwards hanged himself, and which is still known as " Morrison's room ". According to popular tradition, Morrison may still be seen o' nights treading with ghostly footsteps the spiral staircase.

Chapel of Garioch is a long parish in which, in pre-Reformation days, there were three places of worship, Chapel, Logie **Chapel of Garioch.** Durno, and Fetternear. It is only with the last named district that we are concerned in this chapter, but we give the principal estates, with their owners, in the whole parish : Balquhain, Charles S. Leslie ; Blairdaff, Lady Gordon-Cathcart ; Blairdaff and Braco, Francis R. Gregson ; Inveramsay, Elizabeth L. Collie and William L. Collie ; Legatesden, James White ; North Inveramsay, James Murray ; Lethenty, Lieut.-Col. John G. Skene ; Logie Elphinstone, Baird's Trustees as bondholders—Colonel Sir Robert Græme Elphinstone-Dalrymple, Bart., actual proprietor ; Afforsk, Sir Arthur H. Grant, Bart. ; Pitcaple, Henry Lumsden ; Pittodrie, Henry W. Knight Erskine ; and Manar and Harlaw, Henry Gordon.

Fetternear House has been the residence of the Leslies of Balquhain for centuries. Frequently altered and enlarged, it has become one of the largest and finest mansions in the valley. The private grounds extend for about two miles along the river, and are so magnificently wooded that they form quite a feature in the landscape as seen from Kemnay. An old portion of the house was known as the Wallace Tower, there being a tradition that Sir William Wallace spent a night there. Fetternear was a summer residence of the Bishops of Aberdeen, Bishop Alexander Kininmonth having built it in 1329. It had a chapel believed to have dated from 1109, which is referred to in a charter granted by Malcolm IV. in 1160. The ruins of an old chapel and the burial ground are within the grounds ; a place of worship of the old faith has recently been erected near by.

Between Cot-town Wood (485 feet) and Aquithie (423 feet) the river runs in a picturesque "narrow" known as the Garples.

The Inverurie (South) road and the branch from Kintore meet short of Kirktown of Kemnay, and form the South Donside road. After passing through the village of Kemnay it enters Monymusk where Bridge of Ton is crossed, and, keeping a little to the South of the village, rounds Tillyfourie Hill, where it is joined by the road from Aberdeen to Alford *via* Skene.

> Monymusk shall be a buss
> To draw the dun deer doon.

Monymusk. A traveller suddenly set down on the platform of Monymusk station could have very little idea of the beautiful scenery which Kirktown Wood conceals. We find ourselves here on one of the most lovely stretches of the river ; nature has done much for Monymusk, both parish and estate, and the proprietors have not neglected their opportunities. Here we have wood and river, haugh and gorge, hill and rock, to satisfy the mere lover of nature and to attract visitors from a distance ; but the ecclesiologist, the antiquarian, and the historian are also interested. In our journey up the river-side we have found that almost every mile of the valley abounds in incident ; and certainly many centuries ago Monymusk was a centre of "light and leading". Probably it was not then more beautiful than now, for latterly art has stepped in and improved nature. We have now entered on a hilly portion of the valley ; here the river is bounded by two short ranges—the Menaway on the South and Bennachie on the North—which may be said to give zest to the scenery. Exception may be taken to calling Bennachie a "range", but it is not unworthy of that term when its long line of tops stretching from East to West is considered ; nor is the former less worthy to be considered as such with Pitfichie Hill (1244 feet), Cairn William, (1469 feet), Green Hill (1307 feet), and Tillyfourie Hill (874 feet) lying in a South-westerly direction.

The ecclesiastical history of Monymusk is much more ancient than its civil—not that that is a great peculiarity. Here in Culdee times devoted men, the predecessors of the modern missionary, went forth to spread light and civilization in the dark regions of the Garioch and the North, and their sacred places doubtless became the sites of later churches. In those days probably most of the inhabitants were little less barbarous than the natives we seek to Christianise in "darkest Africa". About 1200 the Earl of Mar gifted to the Priory of Monymusk the churches of Alford, Leochel, Invernochty and Rathen ; while the Durward—of whom mention occurs so frequently in "Deeside"— a few years thereafter confirmed a yearly grant made by his grandfather and mother of ten bolls of malt and

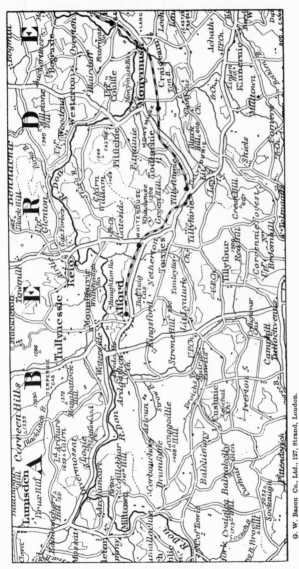

W. JOLLY & SONS, PUBLISHERS, ABERDEEN.

G. W. Bacon & Co., Ltd., 127, Strand, London.

[Face p. 94.

ten stones of cheese. The Priory contained an oratory, a dining room and a dormitory, with several gardens and a croft as well as pasturage, no fewer than six horses being kept by the officials, of whom there must have been a large staff, who were presided over by a Prior in conformity with the constitution of the Augustinian Priory of S. Andrews. The present church tower, and two Norman arches within the building, are memorials of the past. " The church", according to " The View of the Diocese of Aberdeen", " one of the handsomest country churches in Scotland, is about 500 ells West of the house of Monymusk, but by whom, or when built, whether it was the parochial church, or the church of the Priory hard by it, is entirely uncertain, there being no date about it to instruct the one, or records yet heard of to determine the other. About twenty yards North-east of the church are to be discerned the remains of the Priory, now entirely demolished. By what can be discovered of the plan thereof, it appears to have been a large building, and situate on a fruitful soil ".

The Priory is said, according to Hector Boece, to have been founded about 1080 by Malcolm Canmore when proceeding on a military expedition against the people of Moray. He vowed during a halt at Monymusk that should he succeed in the North he would devote the little village to S. Andrew, and found and endow a Priory there. Canmore returned victorious and the Priory was duly established. There were later royal visits to Monymusk ; an entry in the Exchequer Rolls under date 21st April, 1360, shows that £6 13s. 4d. was paid to a burgess of Aberdeen for a cask of wine carried to Monymusk for the use of David II. According to Monday (" From the Tone to the Don", 1886) : " The ruins of this ancient building were finally dug up in 1726, the ornamental stones having been used from time to time towards embellishing Monymusk House. The site of the fish ponds is plainly seen, and, although now forming a portion of the park, their shape is still preserved ". Only the threshold stone now remains in its place, but it has been suggested that other buildings have shared in the stones of the Priory—the enlargement of the church and the manse. Monday had special opportunities for investigation ; nevertheless Sir Arthur H. Grant, disputes several of his statements— pointing out in particular, that the so-called fish ponds were dug by Mr. Robert Grant, who died about 1860 !

The present church is a plain substantial structure, but the massive tower at the West is very conspicuous and striking. The spire was taken down in 1890 as it was in a dangerous condition, when also the present Norman battlements were erected by Sir Arthur H. Grant. The entrance in the tower is singularly small, and is a pure Norman doorway. The lower part of the tower is vaulted, and on entering the church another Norman arch is passed under. At the West end of the church is a beautiful and elaborate Norman chancel-arch. All this fixes the date of the church as certainly as if it were

engraved on the walls, and carries one directly back to the time
of fair Margaret.

The spiritual welfare of Monymusk was as minutely looked
after as in other Donside parishes in pre-reformation days.
Besides *the* church there were three chapels, one at Balvack
near Ton Burn, another West of the site of the Toll-house of
Tillyfourie, and another at Abersnithock, now Braehead,
dedicated to S. Ffinan, a Welsh saint, and still enclosed with
beeches. An interment was made there so recently as 1775.

The lands of Monymusk passed in 1549 to Duncan, the son
of William Forbes of Corsindae. In 1712 the Forbeses sold the
estate to Sir Francis Grant of Cullen, a younger branch of the
Grants of Grant. He had been created a baronet in 1705, and
in 1706 became a Senator of the College of Justice under the
title of Lord Cullen. The latter title is still preserved in the
parish in " Lord Cullen's School ".

Monymusk House is beautifully situated on the right bank
of the river, and is a large, ancient mansion, with a massive
square keep, the central tower of which is 80 feet in height.
Wings have been added to the original building from time to
time ; the castellated appearance of the whole has an imposing
effect. The principal approach is lined by magnificent beeches.
The house contains a very fine collection of paintings by the
old masters and their pupils—including Raphael, Rubens,
Vandyke, Rembrandt, Pousssin, and Correggio. There are
also many valuable books, as well as interesting relics, found in
the parish, the principal of which is "a very beautiful and very
remarkable reliquary" supposed to have belonged to the Priory.
A Moorish gold coin, about the size of a Rose Noble, dated
1097, was found in the churchyard in 1823, and is preserved in
the Library. It had probably been buried with a crusader, or
a pilgrim who had passed through Spain. East of the house,
on the Home Farm, is Campfield, one of the places where it is
said Bruce's army lay encamped previous to the battle of
Inverurie. Here, as in other parts of the Don, pearls have
been found.

Pitfichie Castle is a fine ruin on the left, about half way
between the House and Paradise. Pitfichie forms part of the
estate of Monymusk, to which indeed it anciently belonged.
It was in the possession of the family of Hurry, or Urry, in the
17th century. The last laird of that name, Sir John Urrie,
a general in the Covenanting army, was defeated by Montrose
at Auldearn and Alford in 1645. After the latter defeat he
retired with his broken forces to Pitfichie, where several of the
wounded died and were buried in the vicinity—traces of their
interment were found a few years ago. General Urrie, like
many political characters of the period, changed sides several
times, but to little ultimate advantage, for he was hanged at
Montrose in 1650 while in the royal service. William Forbes,
the young laird of Monymusk, who married, about the end of
the century, Lady Jean, eldest daughter of the first Earl of

Monymusk House

Kintore, brought his young bride to Pitfichie Castle. The
following verses are all that remain of a ballad of which she is
the reputed heroine :—

> " Hoo dee ye like Pitfichie,
>   Hoo like ye there to dwall ;
> Hoo dee ye like Pitfichie,
>   Gentle Jean o' Keith-hall " ?

> " Oh, weel I like Pitfichie,
>   An' I like there to dwall ;
> Oh, weel I like Pitfichie,
>   But nae half sae weel's Keith-hall ".

> " Oh, ye'll get wine an' wa'nuts,
>   An' servants aye at yer call,
> An' young Monymusk to dawt ye ;
>   Ye had na that at Keith-hall ".

> " Oh, I had wine an' wa'nuts,
>   An' servants aye at my call,
> An' the bonny Laird o' Fyvie
>   To see me at Keith-hall ".

The outer walls of Pitfichie Castle, which are from five to
six feet in thickness, appear as sound as ever. The principal
entrance is flanked by two guard rooms, through the walls of
which there are perforated holes, there being holes also above
the doorway through which molten lead could be poured upon
besiegers. In the centre is a large baronial hall ; the upper
part is reached by a spiral stone staircase now in a ruinous
condition. A ghost in a red night-cap formerly haunted the
ruins. A bowman in the castle sent, according to tradition, a
well-directed shaft at an enemy crossing the river at the ford, a
distance of about 400 yards. Human bones, probably of this
"enemy", were actually found about 1885, near the river and
on the traditional site of the burial. Bones have also been
recently found in the school play-ground, near the church, and
in other spots in the vicinity. In the "good old days" thieves
had short shrift, and were buried where most convenient. The
last Highland raiders who visited Monymusk are said to have
"lifted" the cattle at Tombeg. The Laird, with his men,
pursued them on horseback, overtaking the caterans, with their
spoil, in the pass of Tillyfourie. Although hereditary jurisdiction
had long been abolished, the Laird duly tried the reivers and
hung them all at once.

The village once boasted of a distillery, and for long the
"Grant Arms" gave welcome to the passing stranger. Another
local industry, which did not flourish long, was glass-works at
Enzian on the North side of the river.

The popular resort of Monymusk and its visitors is Paradise.
The lairds commenced the planting of trees in 1716, the second
baronet planting no fewer than fifty millions. His successors

have been by no means remiss in improving a beautiful—but what was originally considered an unpromising—estate. Paradise, about two miles from the house, was laid out as a landscape garden in 1719. Many of the pines are now of almost gigantic proportions, but stately and beautiful withal, while leafy beeches afford a delightful shade. The river bounds one side of this earthly Paradise, which the Queen has twice visited—need more be said to indicate its beauties? Vandals are not, alas, wanting even in these days when there is no escaping education; and the generosity of Sir Arthur H. Grant in allowing the public the "freedom" of Paradise has been too often abused, and necessary restrictions have had to be imposed. In addition to evil disposed hands the woods now suffer from the squirrel, the larch disease, and latterly a disease among spruces and silver firs. The squirrel, that lively little animal whom it is such a pleasure to watch among the trees, is unfortunately a serious pest in Monymusk, where he has ruined hundreds of acres of thirty-year-old wood, though a constant warfare is waged against him by the foresters. The capercailzie came to Monymusk in 1888, and has multiplied exceedingly. The red deer pays only an occasional visit to the district; probably the finest and oldest head (c. 1796) adorns Monymusk House.

Between the village and Pitfichie Castle we have "New" Paradise on the left, a shady retreat, however, which is not to be compared with the older plantation near Ord Mill.

Rev. John Skinner, the author of "Tullochgorum", was for some time a schoolmaster in Monymusk; we give the first and last verses of his "Christmas Ba'ing", a poem of thirty-three stanzas :—

> Has ne'er in a' this country been,
>   Sic shoudering and sic fa'ing,
> As happen'd but few ouks sin syne,
>   Here at the Christmas Ba'ing.
> At evening syne the fallows keen
>   Drank till the niest day's dawing,
> Sae snell, that some tint baith their een,
>   And cou'd na pay their lawing,
>   Till the niest day.

*   *   *   *   *

> Has ne'er in Monymuss been seen
>   Sae mony weel beft skins ;
> Of a' the bawmen there was nane
>   But had twa bleedy shins.
> Wi' strenzied shouders mony ane,
>   Dreed'd penance for his sins ;
> And what was warst, scoup'd him at e'en,
>   May be to hungry inns,
>   And cauld that day.

The bare rock surface on the top of Menaway range has been scored with numerous grooves, shewing that the ice of the

Don valley had passed E.N.E. The erratics on this little
range are masses and flags of andalusite and knotted schist.
The granite of Cairn William and Pitfichie Hill is mostly grey,
and there is also a tolerably uniform coarse pink rock. As
felspar is the chief constituent of this rock, and exists as large
crystals scattered through a fine-grained base, the rock of Cairn
William may be regarded as a granite porphyry. On Pitfichie
Hill a small drift was cut, previous to 1840, for a short distance
through a reef of quartz, but as the felspar contained iron
operations were at once abandoned. The present proprietor
had specimens analysed with the same result. The quarry was
tested by a Staffordshire firm, who gave it the name of Henley's
Quarry ; but it is known locally as the " China Quarry". Green
Hill is composed of a peculiar rock, grey in colour, massive and
coarse. " It is a cordierite-gniess, resting apparently on the top
of the surrounding granite, which is probably in place at no
great distance from the surface". Many boulders carried from
this neighbourhood have been found scattered at considerable
distances towards the East.

> The river nobly foams and flows,
> The charm of this enchanted ground,
> And all its thousand turns disclose
> Some fresher beauty varying round,
> Nor could on earth a spot be found
> To nature and to me so dear.

The Don is crossed by several fords in Monymusk, and there
is also a private foot-bridge between Ord Mill on the South
bank and Ramstone on the North. This bridge is at present,
by the courtesy of the owners, open to the public. The river
scenery between Ramstone and the Bridge of Keig is of the
loveliest description, but utterly unknown to the casual Donside
visitor. For the road in these parts on the left bank of the
river is not a leading thoroughfare, yet as it winds with the
river, and openings in the woods disclose varying beauties, the
pedestrian is rewarded with a series of unexpected and charming
views.

Proceeding up the river from Ramstone, the parish of Oyne
is soon entered, its South border being the Don, its North (for
some distance) the Ury. Bennachie, which
gives so much character to the scenery of
Oyne. the Don valley, stands between these two
streams, and its Mither Tap (1698 feet) is a
well-defined peak, over-looking, in rocky dignity, Monymusk
and its vicinity. Three other tops may also be named here—
Craig Shannoch (c. 1600 feet), Oxen Craig (1733 feet), and
Watch Craig (1619 feet). Craig Shannoch appears to the
best advantage from the North, and even Oxen Craig, though
the highest top, is not so popular or so out-standing as Mither
Tap. These tops are all in Oyne, but Watch Craig is at the
meeting point of Oyne, Keig, and Premnay, and is most
prominent as viewed from the South. Millstone Hill (1340

feet), also in Oyne, is a spur of Bennachie, well seen from the valley of the Don. The name is derived from millstones (of red granite) formerly quarried on the hill.

> To thee, sky-mantled Peak ! that lookest down
>> Upon the subject lands, the eyes have turn'd
>> Of many generations, thoughts have burn'd
>> Within the breasts of myriads forced to own
>> A sense of admiration, not unknown
>> To him that sees and feels thee now a charm
>> Telling of that Existence whose dread arm
> Upheav'd thee at the first ! A burnished crown
>> Rests on thy craggy brow, what time thy shade,
>> Advancing death-like, shrouds the sombre plain,
>> Or swift receding bids Morn's light invade
> The flowery fields and Nature live again.
> Thou look'st a Monarch, and thy vision brings
> Flooding upon the soul speechless imaginings.

No mountain in Aberdeenshire—or, indeed, in the North of Scotland—is better known or more frequently visited than Bennachie. Its graceful outline ; its comparative isolation and prominent position ; the magnificent prospect of mountain and lowland scenery to be obtained from its summits ; its easiness of access—all contribute to render Bennachie familiarly known even to those who are not addicted to mountain-climbing. The surrounding district is also of considerable interest, abounding as it does in old castles and other relies of antiquity, such as the Maiden Stone and the Hill Fort—still unsolved problems to antiquaries—in addition to the great battlefield of Harlaw. Moreover, its songs and ballads possess such a powerful hold upon the natives of the district, scattered over the world, that they can never forget

> Whar' Gadie rins, whar' Gadie rins,
> At the back o' Bennachie.

The Maiden Stone stands a little to the North-west of the church of Chapel of Garioch, the Hill Fort encircles Mither Tap. Mither Tap may be readily reached from the Don by a cart-track on the South bank of Birks Burn. The mountain of the Garioch is described at length in "Bennachie", (2nd Ed. 1897).

The picturesqueness of the crags which crown the summit of Bennachie is caused by the tabular weathering of the coarser bands of rock along horizontal joints, the whole of the rock, from the abundance of felspar, decomposing readily. The rock is a typical pink or flesh-coloured granite, composed of orthoclase felspar, quartz, and black or dark brown biotite. Quarry Hill, at the head-streams of Birks Burn, is also known as the English Quarry, because about eighty years ago it was worked by an English company, the granite blocks being sent to Sheerness for dock-building purposes. This quarry has long been disused, but others have been opened on the North side of the hill.

The Don at Tillyfour

Place of Tillyfour will be passed on the left on the way to Birks Burn; the plantations are extensive and varied. It belonged at one time to the Earl of Mar. The mansion which now replaces the old house is a handsome modern erection, commanding a fine river prospect. It is interesting to note that Mr. Gregson of Tillyfour has in his residence a statue of the Blessed Virgin, known as Our Lady of Monymusk, which, before the Reformation, stood in the Priory of Monymusk. This statue, and the one of Our Lady of Aberdeen, are said to be the only two held in veneration before the Reformation which are still in existence. The Monymusk statue is considered by some to be of Spanish or Flemish origin.

The Session records of Oyne date from about the middle of the seventeenth century, and throw interesting side-lights on the manners and customs of the people. In 1663 "Isbel Crombie of Ardiane, ane ignorant fool, was dilated for abusing herself by drunkenness on the Sabbath-day". Next year "John Thomson and his wife" were "challenged for absence from divine worship", and as "the said John had no relevant excuse for himself, ergo, he is ordained to make proffesione of his repentance before the congregatione the next Lord's day, and to pay six shillings and four pence". Stephen Davidsone was the same year, without trial, "excommunicated from the Sacrament of the Lord's Supper, ay, till he give satisfactione, as it is well known that he has been guiltie of witchcraft, in causing dogs to follow him". The good folk who lived under the shadow of Bennachie—whether on Donside or Gadieside—found the ladle a convenient receptacle for otherwise "unpassable money", for on November 12th, 1665, Robert Duncan, "the collector", reported that "ther wer five groats and fourty penny pieces yat would not pass", "in ye poors' box". On April 8th, 1666, "the Sessione agreed with David Tam, wright in Old West Ha, for to build ane stuill of repentance for sax pounds". "Margat Emslie" seems to have paid a substantial penalty for some peccadillo, for on 29th July, 1666, she appeared before the Session and "offered ane bear ruck she had to be forth coming to the use of the Sessione, and gave an plaid worth four pounds qch was given to the officer, and it is ordained that she should enter on the professione of her repentance". Robert Morgan was on 26th May, 1672, "admitted Schoolmaster and Clerk to the Session for the ensuing half year, from the date of the present, and for public reading and precenting in the church; for qch four bolls of victual is to be paid to him of the paroche, with ten pounds of money from the Sessione, and the ordinary colledge fees for teaching any children as shall happen to come to him during the said space". On 16th March, 1673, "the minister and the elders considering how God's worship was molested by dogs in the kirk, desired the collector to cause make ane dog clip", which was duly done and delivered to the officer, at the same time "it was appointed that one of the elders, viz., Patrick Martaine, should wait on the next Lord's day, betwixt the second and third bell, and cause those who brought dogs to the kirk, either themselves or their servants, to take the clip and draw them to the church styll ; and it was ordained that those who disobeyed to do so should be caused satisfie as occasioners of Sabbath breaking ". Another entry shews how "kirk officers" were paid in those days : "John Henrie was elected kirk officer for ensuing half year, and was ordained to get four merks and two pair of shoes in the foresaid time with the other casualities to him, viz., six shillings and eight pennies for every marriage, three shillings and four pennies for every baptisme, thirteen shillings and four pennies for every burial, and three shillings and four pennies for every one charged to the public place of repentance". Probably John found sinners a considerable source of income ! The following entry, dated 1674, is interesting : "the collector ordained to cause make ane caise to the sand glasse"—preacher and dogs alike requiring a certain suppression ! In that year, also, the churchyard dyke was repaired, "it being agreed yt every Heritor, or ane for him, should draw lots qch of them should begin". The following month "intimation was given off ane collection to be gathered next Lord's day for two Christians, Scotsmen born, who were under the Turkish slaverie". On 21st January, 1680, Sabbath breakers were carefully warned ; there must be no buying or selling of goods on that day, or feeing of servants— under the penalty of confiscation of "the money delivered or fee, and the parties punished as said is". Beggars and Egyptians had a hard time in Oyne, for it was intimated that "whosoever ressets beggars should be delet to the Sheriff", and the "Parson did publickly inhibit the people not to resette, harbour, nor entertain the Egyptians so called and in particular the people in Pitmachie, otherways he told them, they might come to further trouble". Little sympathy seems to have been entertained in Oyne for the national (?) musical instrument in the beginning of the eighteenth century : "March 26th, 1701, the Sessione taking into their serious consideration the horrid abuses that are committed at penny bridals to the great dishonour of God, and scandall of the Christian religion ; considering also, that the use of bagpipes doe in a great measure occasion that lascivious and unchristian carriage which is common at marriage feasts, did therefore forbid the same, and whosoever should contraven this enactment forfeits their pledge". In 1717 the "collection" would not appear to have averaged much, for on January 20th, "the said days collection was given to George Thomson for a tow to the Bell". On June 30th of that year, "anent Mary Leslie, the minister reported that she was to appear next Sabbath upon the pillar, and be rebuked, and that she had promised to furnish a sackcloth for herself". Could sincere penitence have gone farther? One circumstance concerning the customs of the previous generation impressed itself on us in our school days ; how the good folks from the neighbourhood of Tillyfour, parishioners of Oyne,

Castle Forbes

regularly crossed Bennachie to church, the more thrifty carrying
their stockings and boots *to be put on as the holy place was
neared.* Church-going dogs remind us of an anecdote of a
Donside clergyman who frequently turned up the glass when
its sand had run out before he had finished his wordy discourse.
Even the patient dogs got weary of his prolonged eloquence,
and so, when the people stood up to the benediction, barked
with delight at their approaching freedom. The worthy
clergyman bore the implied canine reproof as best he could,
for indeed the dogs were not to be restrained ; but at last he
fell upon a simple expedient to secure quietness to the very end
of the service. " Brethren ", said he, " just keep your seats
when I pronounce the benediction, *and cheat the dogs* ".

The principal estates, with their owners, in Oyne, are :
Ardoyne, Trustees of the late Robert Grant ; Logie Elphinstone,
Baird's Trustees as Bondholders—Colonel Sir Robert Græme
Elphinstone-Dalrymple, Bart., actual proprietor ; Pittodrie,
Henry W. K. Erskine ; Tillyfour, Francis R. Gregson ;
Petmathan, Major Thomas Leith ; Westhall, Mrs. Leith ; and
Drumrossie, Trustees of the late William Leslie.

Birks Burn crossed, the traveller is in the parish of Keig. The
principal estates, with their owners, are : Castle Forbes, Lord
Forbes ; Brindy, Charles E. N. Leith-Hay;
Keig. Balgowan, Trustees of the late Robert C.
Grant ; and Whitehouse, William S.
Farquharson. After crossing Birks Burn,
the road passes through Glenton, and then enters a gorge with
the descriptive name of My Lord's Throat.

In the " good old days " Keig was much associated with
Monymusk, for the parish was merely church-lands belonging
to the Priory. When the Culdees were made landless their
possessions passed to the Canons Regular of S. Andrews, and
so the Bishop of S. Andrews sat in Parliament as Lord Keig
and Monymusk. The oldest known place of worship had been
on the left bank of the river, now within the grounds of Castle
Forbes, where there is a graveyard with the remains of a church.
Here also is the burial vault of the Forbeses of Castle Forbes.

Castle Forbes, the seat of Lord Forbes, the premier Baron
of Scotland, is the outstanding mansion ; situated at an
elevation of 490 feet above sea level on the South-western slope
of Bennachie, it occupies a conspicuous position as seen from
many points in the Valley. Built of granite in the old baronial
castellated style, it is a large and handsome structure designed
by the late Mr. Archibald Simpson. The old house was
known as Putachie. The grounds are extensive, and there are
numerous plantations clothing the slopes of Bennachie in the
vicinity. Early in the 16th century, Lord Forbes had been
of no small service to the citizens of Aberdeen in defending
their rights to the river fishings, and the magistrates were not
ungrateful. We have already seen how these worthy aldermen
paid substantial compliments when acknowledging obligations ;

in this case the Baron was rewarded with a tun of wine. But, alas, it was found that latterly my Lord, while he accepted the wine from Bonaccord, fished for salmon "in undue time", and so the claret was withdrawn. Lord Forbes complained, insisting that the wine was a right, and he was backed up by his men, who "descended" in 1530 in Highland style on Aberdeen. They returned home without horses or arms ; nevertheless the old friendly relations were soon re-established, and the citizens named the locality where Lord Forbes's town-house was situated Putachie-side. The tenth baron served with distinction under Gustavus Adolphus and was a man of affairs, and the celebrated Duncan Forbes of Culloden belonged to a branch of the Putachie family.

In the Wood of North-Keig is The Barmkyn (929 feet). The summit is a fort or camp, somewhat reminding one of the Echt example. There is a loose heap of stones in the centre, with a circular enclosure of stones about 80 yards in diameter. On Cothiemuir Hill, on the North side of the Home Farm, there is a stone circle 25 yards in diameter ; it seems to have consisted originally of 11 upright stones and an altar stone, the latter about 14 feet long.

The Bridge of Keig, which crosses the Don at the South-west corner of the Castle grounds, was built in 1817 ; it is a graceful arch of 101 feet span.

The parish of Cluny, though it does not touch the river, is a close neighbour to Kemnay and Monymusk, the Ton Burn separating it from the latter. A road leaves **Cluny.** the Aberdeen and Alford turnpike near Linton House, and, passing Cluny Castle, leads directly to Monymusk. The parish includes the half of Kinnernie, which was annexed about 1743, the other half being added to Midmar, but the Donside tourist is mainly concerned with three castles—Castle Fraser, Cluny Castle and Tillycairn Castle, near the North boundary of the parish.

The ancient name of Castle Fraser was Muchal, or Muchil-in-Mar, a name still preserved by Muchal Burn, on the North of the castle, a tributary of the Don. The castle is one of the most interesting in the Don valley, being conspicuous for the variety of its main features and its long rambling irregular masses. It is rich in modelling and carved decoration, and is said by experts to be one of the finest specimens of the Flemish style of architecture in Scotland. The oldest part of the building is a square tower, which dates from the 15th century ; the oldest incribed date is 1576. It has a "lug" for overhearing conversation. A round tower is the most striking feature ; it is 100 feet in height, and has a massive balustrade of granite. The castle had an unpleasant visit from Montrose and his forces on 14th October, 1644.

The Frasers of Castle Fraser came from Corntoun (see page 30) ; in 1633 Andrew Fraser was created Lord Fraser, but the title became extinct in 1720. In "Miss Bristow's Wood", within the grounds, there is a monument erected to the memory of that lady, who was aunt of the third Lord Lyttleton. Miss Bristow was an intimate friend of Miss Fraser's, and died at the Castle—hence the monument. One part of the inscription reads (in Latin): "Farewell! Alas, how much less is the society of others than the memory of thee". There are some fine old ash trees in the grounds, as well as numerous firs of large size.

Cluny Castle was originally built by Sir Alexander Gordon, one of the Huntly family, in the 15th century. It was rebuilt in 1836-40, and is an imposing and magnificent structure furnished with exquisite taste. The old building had, in 1794, "a double barred iron gate, weighing thirty-two stone, with many iron bolts, and the remains of a fosse, once full of water"—the disappearance of the gate has been much lamented by some. The new building is of a fine grey granite, beautifully dressed. An addition, made in 1872, includes a private chapel, which is fitted up in a gorgeous style of church architecture. The floor is laid with rich encaustic tiles, and seated with dark carved oak benches; and the open oak roof rests upon faint pink-coloured polished Corrennie granite pilasters profusely ornamented with gilded cornices and scrolls. The most striking features on the front main building are the corridor and staircase, which are unusually large. The castle, which is seventeen miles from Aberdeen by road, is surrounded by extensive grounds, which contain some of the best specimens of beech, ash, elm, plane, lime, oak and birch trees— many of great size and highly ornamental. A Pinetum was formed in 1869; it contains about four hundred varieties of ornamental trees and evergreen shrubs. The Mausoleum stands on the site of the old parish church.

In 1449 James II. gave a grant of Cluny to the first Earl of Huntly, since which date the lands have remained in the hands of the Gordons.

Tillycairn Castle, which stands to the West of Cluny Castle, is a ruin which may be seen from the railway. Formerly it belonged to Matthew Lumsden, the author of a history of the family of Forbes, of the Cushnie Lumsdens, who died in 1580— and that is about all there is to tell concerning it.

Tillyfourie station is in Monymusk, but almost touches Cluny and is also within a mile of the borders of Tough. Here also,

Tillyfourie. as already stated, the Aberdeen and Alford turnpike is joined by the South Donside road. Granite quarries have been opened on both sides of the railway, which here runs through a defile, at the West end of which the Vale of Alford is entered. The quarries on the right are on the slope of Tillyfourie Hill, those on the left are on Corrennie, the latter being in Cluny. The Corrennie quarries are about 300 feet above the level of the station, and there two distinct varieties of granite are found side by side—the ordinary blue and the pink, of which latter stone, it may be mentioned, the Aberdeen Art Gallery and Gray's School of Art are built.

The Red Hill (1605 feet) of Corrennie is a common term for the hill generally. Besides that top (which is at the meeting point of three parishes—Cluny, Kincardine o' Neil and Tough), two others may be named, Green Hill (1607 feet) and Benaquhallie (1621 feet). The higher ground, known as Corrennie Forest, was a Commonty, but was divided in 1835-42.

VII.—THE VALE OF ALFORD.

It is years, lang-gane years, since I last saw the place,
But nae distance nor time can remembrance efface ;
The loved scenes of my boyhood, the dear Donside braes,
The kirk, the deaf bellman, the young laird's spankin' greys,
The reid smiddy, the smith (baith oor Vet. and precentor—
Hoo we sang roon his fire in the cauld days o' winter !)—
I can see them a' yet, but there's naething mair plain
Than the laigh thacket school o' auld Martha Macbain.

THE Vale of Alford is confined by gentle slopes on both sides of the river ; on the East it is cut off from the strath by Bennachie, the Menaway range and Corrennie, and is confined on the West by Coillebhar Hill and Lord Arthur's Cairn—the last named a summit of the Correen Hills. The Eastern barrier of the Vale is rather pronounced, and may be said to be pierced at two points only—where the Don has cut a way between Bennachie and Cairn William, and where road and railway enter by the "slack" between Tillyfourie Hill and Green Hill. The Vale thus embraces parts of the following parishes : Alford, Tullynessle-Forbes, Tough and Keig ; though the Vale proper is perhaps only the lower-lying ground on both banks of the river between the natural East and West boundaries. The Vale is agriculturally rich and naturally beautiful—quite equal to the Garioch in the one, and much superior in the other. Alford, the centre of the district, has an added importance as being the terminus of the railway, and as a consequence the village has much increased and improved within recent years. It now caters for the summer visitor, a sure indication that the travelling public has at last acknowledged that the middle reaches of the Don are worthy of a place in its "preferred list". Alford is an excellent centre for a holiday, long or short ; there are objects of interest all around, and in summer and autumn the hills and woods, of which there is no lack, are delightful.

The Vale embraces an area of about fifteen square miles of alluvium, overlying granite, and this is the geological explanation of its fertility. The Vale had probably been at some remote period a series of marshes and shallow lochans. "The river, with its modern terraces, occupies a narrow belt 40 to 50 feet below the general level of the plain, and this, with the narrow valley cut further to the East of the river Don, between Bennachie and Cairn William, forms a typical example of gorge and plain. A similar case occurs to the East of Monymusk, where the Don, after passing through the broad haughlands of Nether Coullie, is confined between steep boulder-clay banks from Kemnay to Inverurie".

The railway comes to a " dead end " at the village, or more correctly speaking, the village has been erected East and West of the station. Built of the beautiful granite

Alford.

for which the Vale is celebrated, the little capital of the district has a smart appearance, and the population is steadily, if slowly, increasing. The goods traffic at the station is considerable, apart from the fact that during the past quarter of a century an immense quantity of wood from the upper part of Donside has been despatched by rail. The business centre of the parish in old times—if the local commercial element had any existence in those days—had been about two miles to the Westward, in the neighbourhood of the church and the muir. There is no lack of roads converging on the village : due North to Montgarrie and Tullynessle ; Westward (crossing an old road from Deeside to the North) to the church whence a Parliamentary Commissioners' road holds Southward by Leochel Burn ; while Eastward there is the Aberdeen turnpike. The Westward road, at the crossing, also holds at right angles for the river, which it crosses at Bridge of Alford and thence proceeds up the left bank ; there is no main road on the other side West of the church. North from Bridge of Alford the parliamentary road leads through Tullynessle, and there are also several local roads.

At the cross-roads just mentioned the distances are :—

Miles.		Miles.	
⅝	Church of Alford.	13½	Deeside Road (Dess).
4	Scuttrie, Leochel.	1¼	Alford Station.
8	Cross Roads, Lumphanan.	3	Old Military Road,
14½	Tarland.		Muggarthaugh.

The principal estates, with their owners, in the parish are : Haughton, Miss Farquharson ; Asloun, James S. Forbes ; Tillychetly, Henry O. D. Davidson ; Carnaveron, William F. C. Stewart ; Kingsford, Charles L. Grant ; and Breda, Neil McLean.

The church (enlarged in 1826) was built in 1804 on the site of a chapel dedicated to S. Andrew, which bore the date 1603. About the beginning of the 13th century the church of Alford was given by the Earl of Mar to the Priory of Monymusk. A monument which had stood in the pre-Reformation church, and fragments of which have been preserved, bears the following inscription :—

> Within this isle inter'd behind these stones,
> Are pious, wise, good Mary Forbes' bones ;
> To Balfluig daughter, and of blameless life,
> To Mr. Gordon, Pastor here, the wife.

Expiravit Apr : 27, A.D. 1728, Æt. suæ 46.

Another stone, dated 1759, praises in rhyme another lady :—

> Here lys below this stons,
> Pious, wirtus, Iean Wisharts bons,

Wife to John Bain
Some time in Bridgend
Of Knockandoch.
All that was dicent & descret,
Did in her parts & in her person meet ;
She mead appear thro hir wnbilemeshd life,
The tender & the loving wife.

A plain head-stone, dated 1724, gives as the residence of the deceased, " Hoodhouse of Alfoord", thus reminding us of an old name. Hoodhouse or Headhouse is an old term for an hostelry ; it was generally (as in this instance) near the church. Two antiquities may be noted in the vicinity of the church : the Roundabout, the site of a fort or camp having an area of about an acre ; and Damil (725 feet), a larger camp. Owing to the crowded state of the churchyard a cemetery was recently opened near the village.

A battle was fought in Alford on 2nd July, 1645, between Montrose and the Covenanters under Baillie. The battle-field, which was on and around the Latch Howe, lies between the North-west end of the village and the 26th mile-stone, the road there now passing through a wood. On the East side is Feight Faulds, doubtless associated with the combat ; on the East side of Tough, immediately to the West of Boglouster Wood, is Bloody Faulds, where it is said some of the retreating and defeated Covenanters were overtaken and killed. This battle is memorable as a success in the failing cause of Charles, which for a time gave the king's friends renewed hope. Montrose, after gathering his forces at Corgarff, marched to meet Baillie at Keith, but, failing to draw him into an engagement there, withdrew Southward, and latterly manœuvred him into a fight at Alford. On 2nd July, 1645, the opposing forces were in sight, Baillie on the North and Montrose on the South of the Don near the ford at Montgarrie. It was part of Montrose's plan to get Baillie to cross, and for this purpose part of his force was concealed ; and finally, it is said against his better judgment, Baillie crossed the ford and passed over some rough ground and a piece of boggy land and then was met by Montrose. The battle raged fiercely for some time without much success being gained by either side ; but eventually the Covenanting horse were repulsed by the cavalry on the other side, who quickly enveloped the rear of Baillie's force, and the fight became a rout.   In the final charge Lord George Gordon, eldest son of the Marquis of Huntly, who was leading the king's forces, was mortally wounded, and his loss was deplored by the whole army and by none more than by Montrose. The numbers engaged were probably about 2000 foot on each side, with 600 horse under Baillie and about half that number with Montrose. The body of Lord Gordon was carried to Old Aberdeen and interred with great pomp " hard by his mother". The " Gordon Stone", where Lord Gordon fell, is still pointed out ; it is about 125 yards above the road, and a quarter of a mile short of the

26th milestone. Almost covered with blaeberry bushes, and only about two feet above ground, it is not readily noticed. The upper surface is about six feet square.

At Ardgathan, between the battle-field and the church, is a circle known as the Auld Kirk—a name suggestive of a former use of the spot. The Gallow Hill is in the vicinity—the parish had thus evidently in the good old times not been without the usual appurtenances of a high civilization ! Alford was an ancient barony and the court was as shrewd as the royal burghs lower down the river in securing obedience to its decrees : " The said day it is statut and ordainit, be ye laird and bailzie, that the masteris of the cotters, girsmen, and others, servents that dwells with them, sal be obleight for yeir servents ; and gif they pey nocht their maisters, they sall be pyndit for the dowbill, betwixt this and the daye aught dayes, of ye levie and transport moneyis, and the poyndis to be delyverit to ye maisteris, and never to be relievyit agane ".

Alford boasted of two castles, Balfluig and Asloun. The former is on the right bank of Buckie Burn, near the village ; the latter on the left bank of Leochel Burn. Balfluig is a tall keep, but the building wherein barony courts were held is now associated with agriculture. The date (1556) is inscribed over the door. The first Forbes of Balfluig (see page 78) was John of the Corsindae family ; another John sold the lands in 1753, and is said to have gone to Holland. John Philip, the celebrated Aberdeen artist, is connected with the laird of 1720. This laird left a small annual sum for the parish schoolmaster, and the holder of that office in 1854 had a portrait of the benefactor painted by Philip, who was then, along with his friend Sterling, painting studies in the school-room of Alford, during the " hairst play ", for their respective pictures of " The Collecting of the Offering ", and " The Sermon ". Little remains of Asloun Castle ; among its fragments an angle tower with shot holes still stands. According to " The Statistical Account ", the building was square in form, with two round towers. The first storey was vaulted, and in one of the vaults there was a well. Montrose is said to have spent a night at Asloun previous to the battle of Alford.

Haughton House is finely situated, surrounded by woods, on the right bank of the river, North from the village. The first Farquharson (1721) of Haughton, was John Farquharson in Breda ; and a successor in 1753 acquired the lands and barony of Alford. Miss Farquharson is thus superior of the village. Breda, originally called Broadhaugh, is about two miles West from the village ; its mansion, which is built in the old Scottish style, has a charming situation, with an old beech avenue leading to the river. There is a family mausoleum, surrounded by a cluster of trees, near the Don, where the first Farquharson of Breda was interred. He was a son of the laird of Cluny (Braemar) who was locally known as "the meikle factor of Invercauld ". A little to the West of the mausoleum, the Don runs over a rock bottom for about a quarter of a mile, particularly at Poundash Falls.

Carnaveron Hill (865 feet) overlooks the village of Alford on the North. On the summit of this hill were found several stone coffins, with an urn containing bones and ashes. The cairn at one time was 125 feet in diameter and 25 feet high. Eastward of Carnaveron Hill is Strone Hill (950 feet), the summit of which Miss Farquharson of Haughton cleared of trees in 1896. The fallen stones of an old circle were then discovered and placed upright ; there were 16 stones, and an altar stone at the South-west side of the circle, which had a diameter of about 21 yards. There had possibly been an inner circle also. The enclosed space had been at one time paved with rough stones, but most of them had been removed to form a cairn close by. Seven ancient graves were found during the clearing operations.

The botanical world owes not a little to the late John Duncan, a humble weaver at Droichsburn on the borders of Leochel. He was "discovered" by Mr. Jolly, one of H.M. Inspectors of Schools, with the result that over £300 was subscribed for the old enthusiast, who had scoured to some effect the hills and glens of his district. He did not enjoy the public's generosity many months, and on his death left his herbarium to Marischal College.

The principal estates, with their owners, in the parish of Tough are : Tonly, George Moir Byres ; Whitehouse, William Farquharson ; Tillyfour, the Trustees of the late Francis Buchan ; and Tullochvenus, John Adam. Tillyfour, formerly tenanted by and afterwards belonging to the late Mr. William McCombie, M.P. for West Aberdeenshire, had in that famous breeder's time almost a world-wide reputation. It was then the head-quarters of the best Aberdeen or Angus polled breed of cattle, and was visited by the Queen in 1866 for the special purpose of seeing some of those wonderful animals which had spread abroad Mr. McCombie's fame as a breeder of polled stock.

Tough.

Tonley House is a large old building, standing in a beautiful dell near the church. It is enriched with much that is valuable in antiquities, art and literature. A unique piece of decorative work was recently executed in the hall by Messrs. Hay & Lyall, Aberdeen. The ceiling is panelled, each panel being highly enriched with pendant centres ; on the middle panel are the full arms, with motto, of the family, while the family crests are placed in each of the four corner panels. All round there is a deep festoon frieze in high relief, with centres about four feet apart, on which are emblazoned coats of arms of the various families connected with Moir Byres.

The mansion of Whitehouse stands high (c. 650 feet) on the Western slope of Green Hill (Menaway), and so commands a fine view of the Vale. It is well wooded ; within the plantations there is a private burial ground.

Luath's Stone stands on Green Hill, just within the parish. It is over 12 feet in height, and is evidently monumental. Luath "is said" to have been a son of Macbeth and to have fallen here in his flight from Lumphanan.

There was formerly a great marsh West of Bents Burn, which was partially drained over two hundred years ago. The land is now called Strath, and has practically all been reclaimed.

As in Alford, there is in this parish a circle known as the Auld Kirk.

Whitehouse station is in the parish of Keig, but close to the Northern border of Tough. The distance to Bridge of Keig is 2½ miles ; Insch 9⅝ miles.

Leochel-Cushnie. Leochel has given its own name to its principal stream (or is it *vice versa ?*) which it sends through the parish of Alford from Droichsbridge to the Don ; Cushnie has its own "Glen" ; and so the parish only claims connection with the Vale of Alford as a neighbour overlooking the more fertile Howe. The principal estates, with their owners, in the parish are : Cushnie, Col. Sir William S. Seton ; Brux, Hon. Atholl M. Forbes ; Craigievar, Trustees of Lord Sempill ; Lynturk, Peter D. McCombie ; and Hallhead, Henry Wolridge-Gordon.

The parishes of Leochel and Cushnie were united so recently as 1795. Leochel church was dedicated to S. Marnan, Cushnie to S. Bride ; there were chapels at Lynturk, Corbanchory and Newton of Corse. The Earl of Mar gifted the church and churchlands of Leochel (1165-1170) to the church of S. Mary of Monymusk. The church of the united parishes is on an eminence between the old churches of Leochel and Cushnie, which are both in ruins. That of Leochel has little more than the West gable standing with the belfry ; here the Forbeses of Craigievar have a burial aisle, known as "The Howff". It was in this aisle, according to "The New Statisical Account", that John Forbes, commissary, son of the Bishop of Caithness, was buried in 1668, " at night, with torches ". The following is a quaint rhyming inscription on a tombstone dated 1784 :—

Here lies Peter Milner, a sober man,
Who never us'd to curse nor ban.
Elizabeth Smith, she was his wife,
He had no other all his life.
He died in July, 1784,
Aged 77, or little more.
And she in July, 1779,
Years 53 was her lifetime ;
With Robert and Jean their children dear,
And Elizabeth Milner and Janet Fraser,
Their grandchildren lies here ;
In Rumblie they lived just near by,
And in this place their dust doth lye.

The church of Cushnie, now a picturesque ruin, stood in the

Corse Castle

Glen or Howe, and was covered with heather up to about 1792 ; the oldest inscribed date is 1637, the bell being dated 1686. The site of S. Bride's Well, near the church, is still pointed out. Cushnie is rather an elevated district, for the church was at an altitude of nearly a thousand feet. The climate is necessarily severe : —

> The nor'lan' win' is blawin' snell,
> And Cushnie hills are cauld,
> It's we maun lift an unco prey
> An' syne we'll draw to hauld.

Even Father Blakhal, in his "Brieffe Narratione", says the hills of Cushnie are "as wyld a piece of ground as is in all Brittaine".

Craigievar Castle stands at an altitude of 838 feet on the Eastern slope of Craigievar Hill (1146 feet), on the left bank of Leochel Burn, among stately old ash and beech trees. It is a fine specimen of the Franco-Scottish fortified mansion, being one of the best preserved and characteristic examples of its period. The lands of Craigievar became the property of the Mortimers by charter from James II. in 1457. Roger Mortimer commenced the building of the castle early in the seventeenth century, when the estate was purchased by William Forbes, an ancestor of the present occupant, who completed the building in 1626. The interior of the castle is in keeping with the exterior style, the furnishings and decorations carrying one back over two centuries. The great hall with its gigantic fireplace and its ornamented roof and stuccoed walls, is a fine specimen of the banqueting hall of an ancient baron. Over the great staircase is the legend, "Doe Not Vaiken Sleiping Dogs", with the date 1668 ; the Forbeses were not to be touched with impunity, as may also be understood from a characteristic saying of the time, "I'm a Craigievar man ; who daur trouble me"?

On a farm on the right bank of the Burn of Cushnie was born the late Surgeon Major Shepherd, whose "First Aid to the Wounded" is known to every ambulance pupil. A monument in the Church and the Shepherd Gold Medal in the University perpetuate his name. Cushnie is the native parish of the Lumsdens, whose names are so celebrated throughout Aberdeenshire and elsewhere as liberal, intelligent and enterprising landowners, authors, and soldiers.

Above Craigievar Castle the Leochel Burn is known as the Burn of Corse ; and one of the most interesting scenes in the parish is formed by the hoary ruins of Corse Castle, with at its base this burn, there widened into a lakelet. The divisions and arrangements of parishes in Donside, as in other districts, are sometimes rather puzzling ; as for Corse, it is *quoad civilia* in Coull, but geographically and *quoad sacra* in Leochel-Cushnie. There is a close connection between Corse and Craigievar ; the former castle was built in 1581 by William Forbes, the father of the celebrated Bishop Patrick Forbes and of the founder of the Craigievar family, now represented by Lord Sempill. Tradition says that previously to the building of the Corse strong-hold William Forbes had had his house plundered by Highland caterans, on which he vowed that, please God, he would build a house at which thieves would need to knock ere they entered. His successor, the Bishop, had even a stronger assailant to resist, for the Devil paid him a visit, but being worsted in a religious discussion took a hasty departure. Finding the staircase a rather round-about way of retiring he burst through the wall, part of which he took with him ! Certain marks on the stone steps used to be pointed out in proof of the truth of this tradition. Bishop Forbes died in 1635 and was interred within Dunbar's aisle in S. Machar's Cathedral.

Corse and Craigievar both suffered "great oppressions" in 1636 by seven "notorious limmers", who were ultimately hanged in Edinburgh, their heads being set up in exemplary places. Later in that year, six other "limmers" were similarly dealt with, but yet the "spulzing" did not cease, for in 1644 the laird of Craigievar "transports his haill victuals to Fintray, to be kept from plundering". But in the following century the times were more settled, and the Barony Court of Craigievar had to be reckoned with. In 1711 the officer of Court was ordered to search out all idlers, men and women, so that they might be sent to service ; at the same time servants receiving and masters paying extravagant fees were to be dealt with. The rules of good husbandry were also enforced, and attempts to seek redress at other tribunals were discouraged by a fine of £20 Scots, for "reason was to be got" at the laird's Court. In the case of two quarrelsome neighbours a simple remedy was ordered ; they had to cast lots, and he on whom the lot fell had "to flitt at the next Whitsunday, 1725".

Lynturk Castle, which stood on the borders of Tough, has disappeared altogether, the site being represented by Castle-knowe. The lands of Lynturk became the property of the Irvines about the end of the sixteenth century, and remained in their hands for about one hundred years. A daughter of Irvine of Lynturk married Gordon of Straloch (page 16). The castle was described in 1843 as the most ancient building in the district, though even then the ruins (which were standing in 1793) had disappeared and only a part of the fosse was traceable—now even that has gone.

The Don is the boundary between the parishes of Alford and Tullynessle-Forbes, and it is crossed by two bridges—at Montgarrie and Bridge of Alford. The **Tullynessle-Forbes.** latter, consisting of three arches, dating from 1811, is a graceful structure at a beautiful reach of the river. Formerly there was a ford and a ferry here—the latter known as Boat of Forbes. Bridge of Alford was a place of no small importance in coaching days ; it has again come into favour, and its hotel is much frequented by anglers. The Northern boundary of Tullynessle-Forbes is a range of hills from Bennachie Westward : Knock Saul (1355 feet) and Suie Hill (1362 feet), both on the borders of Leslie, and Correen Hills on the borders of Clatt. The army of the Covenanters lay encamped between Montgarrie and Boat of Forbes the night preceding the Battle of Alford. The principal estates, with their owners, in the parish are : Braes of Forbes, Lord Forbes ; Whitehaugh, Rev. William Forbes Leith ; and Knockespock, Harry G. Fellowes-Gordon. Little John's Length, in the North-eastern corner of the parish, where it touches Leslie and Keig, had at one time a natural " table " where five lairds could sit down, each on his own estate. The proprietors were Lord Forbes, the laird of Whitehaugh, the laird of Balgowan, the laird of Johnstone, and the laird of Leithhall.

The church is on the East side of the Suie Road, near the junction of Suie Burn with Esset Burn. The present building was erected in 1876, of finely dressed Sylavethy granite from the quarry of that name, and shews the extraordinary advance in the architecture of parish churches in comparatively recent times. It has already been noted (page 46) that such churches were often thatched ; the internal arrangements naturally corresponded. Thus the seats in Tullynessle church, in the time of our informant's grandfather, were mere boards placed on turf-piles.

Whitehaugh House, a mansion in the Grecian style of architecture, is to the East of Montgarrie, and, situated in the middle of a fine lawn, faces the river, almost opposite Haughton. Leiths appear to have held the estate of Montgarrie, or Whitehaugh, since about the end of the sixteenth century, an heiress marrying in the beginning of the following century a Forbes of Tolquhon who thereafter assumed the name of Leith. The Knights Templars had large possessions in this parish, as indicated by the names Temple Glen, Temple Close, and S. John's Close. There is a Mausoleum at the West of Temple Glen, erected by Lieut.-Colonel James John Forbes Leith, who died in 1841.

A short distance to the East from Whitehaugh House is a disused ford across the Don, known as Highlander's Ford ; near the house is the Highlander's Haugh. These names are said to owe their origin and to have a reference to the time of the Battle of Harlaw, but more probably the names refer to the crossing of Montrose's army prior to the Battle of Alford. Esset Burn joins the Don close to the village of Montgarrie. The vicinity is rich in antiquities : an Eirde House was found here ; there is also the site of a causeway and a stone circle ; stone cists and ladles have been dug up ; and the name Druidsfield, in the neighbourhood of the stone circle, also points to pre-historic times. There was also a mansion called Whitehouse.

Terpersie (called also Dalpersie) Castle is on the left bank of Esset Burn, a little to the North-west of the church.   It has been described as "meagre in historic association as well as in architectural importance"—and certainly, crowded into a farm steading concealed among trees, it is not now imposing to the stray passers-by.   The building bears the date 1561, with the crest of the Gordons, a boar's head.   The Gordons of Terpersie were a branch of the Gordons of Lesmoir.   The laird at Terpersie was at the battle of Corrichie in 1563.   The castle was burned in 1645 by Baillie's army during his encampment at Montgarrie.   The laird during the rebellion of 1745 joined the army of Prince Charles, and was present at Culloden. Gordon by and by returned to Terpersie, but too soon for safety.   A party of troops was soon on his track, and apprehended him in the castle, from which however his family had previously fled.   But his captors were doubtful of his identity, for not a soul would own to their prisoner being the laird, and so he was dragged to the manse for identification.   On the way there the party passed the temporary residence of Gordon's family, and one of the children recognising their father, exclaimed, "Daddy!   Daddy!"   Another version makes the laird adopt the disguise of a servant in his own castle.   He was standing in the court-yard while a company of red-coats passed by, and the officer asked him if the laird was at home.   The reply was of course in the negative, but one of his children unfortunately called "Father"!   There is even a third version— that he was betrayed by the minister of Kennethmont.   But the result is certain : Gordon lost his head on 15th November, 1746, and his family lost their estate.   Terpersie was thereafter for some time in the possession of the York Buildings Company ; it now forms part of the estate of Knockespock.   General Gordon of Khartoum is said by some authorities to belong to the Terpersie family.

Forbes was united to Tullynessle in 1808.   The roofless church with its crow-stepped ivy-clad gables is a picturesque ruin within a loop of the Don and directly under the shadow of Coillebhar Hill.   Kirkton of Forbes is about two miles West from Bridge of Alford, and its retired situation in an extreme corner of the parish never fails to remind one of how frequently old church buildings have got stranded in the march of modern improvement.   We are also here reminded of the preference of ecclesiastics, in pre-Reformation days, for the river's banks— as witness the sites of S. Machar's Cathedral, and the old churches of New Machar, Dyce, Fintray (Grange and two churches), Kinellar, Kintore, Kinkell, Inverurie (two), Chapel of Garioch (two), Kemnay, Monymusk (Priory and three churches), Keig and Alford.   In most of these instances the sacred buildings are within a few yards of the Don.

The old parish of Forbes crossed the Don at Kirkton, and thus embraced Bithnie with the Eastern slope of Coillebhar Hill.   Four parishes meet on this hill a short distance to the South of the cairn, viz : Alford, Leochel-Cushnie, Kildrummy, and Tullynessle-Forbes. The hill may be easily ascended from Bithnie, the river being crossed by a wooden bridge opposite the entrance to Littlewood Park. The view embraces the following mountain tops—Bennachie, Cairn-mon-earn, Kerloch, Clochnaben, Mount Battock, Mount Keen, Morven, Lochnagar, Ben Avon, Ben Muich Dhui, Cairngorm, Ben Newe, The Buck, Tap o' Noth, Knock Hill, Binn Hill of Cullen, Tillymorgan, Brimmond Hill and the Hill of Fare. The hill, as its name implies, was at one time completely wooded. One of the largest of the Aberdeenshire bonfires commemorative of the Queen's jubilee was on the top of Coillebhar, on which occasion between sixty and seventy others were visible from the summit.

Lord Arthur's Cairn (1699 feet), the highest summit of the Correen Hills, is on the borders of Tullynessle-Forbes and Auchindoir-Kearn. It is immediately opposite Coillebhar Hill, and may be ascended from Littlewood Park. Grassy on the lower slopes, there is heather higher up, the summit being crowned by the ruins of a so-called "summer-house". The name of the hill is strikingly suggestive, but nothing certain is now known of its origin, though probably it refers to some of the combats between the Forbeses and the Gordons. The view from the top is practically identical with that from Coillebhar Hill, with, however, some variations, Mormond Hill, for instance, being visible from the former and not from the latter. Ben Rinnes is also seen from Lord Arthur's Cairn, though, curiously enough, not from the very summit. The view extends, on a clear day, from Cullen to Montrose ; the smoke of Aberdeen may be discerned, though not the city itself, and the sands near Newburgh are also distinguishable. The feature of the view is the prospect of the distant Cairngorms—the long line of Ben Avon, with its rocky protuberances, the shoulder of Ben Muich Dhui, and the crest of Cairngorm ; grandly beautiful if seen on a clear summer day—perhaps more picturesque if seen with patches of snow on them.

A species of mica slate was at one time excavated on the Correen Hills. It was known as "Correen stone", and was largely used for pavement for halls and kitchens. It possessed the curious characteristic of exuding moisture on the approach of wet weather.

THE BATTLE OF ALFORD.

FOUGHT JULY 2, 1646.

The Grahams and Gordons of Aboyne,
    Camp'd at Drummenor bog ;
At the castle there they lay all night,
    And left them scarce a hog.

The black Baillie, that auld dog,
    Appeared in our light :

We quickly raise up frae the bog,
  To Alford march'd that night.

        .   .   .   .

We lay at Lesly all night
  They camped at Asloun ;
And up we raise afore daylight,
  To ding the beggars doun.

        .   .   .   .

Montrose's men cam' marchin' sooth,
  Well-trained and fou' o' skill ;
Three thousan' kilted Hielanmen
  Cam' doon abune Millhill.

Before we was in battle rank,
  We was anent Millhill ;
I wat fell weel they gar'd us rue,
  We gat fighting our fill.

        .   .   .   .

They haunted us, and daunted us,
  They drave us here and there ;
Until three hundred of our men,
  Lay gasping in their lair.

The Earl of Mar the right wing guided,
  The colours stood him by ;
Lord George Gordon the left wing guided
  Who well the sword could ply.

        .   .   .   .

There came a ball shot from the west,
  That shot him thro' the back ;
Although he was our enemy,
  We grieved for his wreck.

We cannot say t'was his own men,
  But yet it came that way ;
In Scotland, their was not a match
  To that man where he lay. *

---

* From Laing's "Thistle of Scotland", 1823, with one verse from tradition. This
fragment, or rather series of fragments, is all that has come down to us of the
traditionary ballad recording the defeat of the Covenanters by Montrose at Alford.—
Like its companion ballad " The Battle of Philliphaugh", it is written from the
Covenanting side. The introduction of " the Earl of Mar " as a leader in the battle,
and the writer or reciter speaking of Baillie, the Covenanting general, as " that auld
dog", are ingrowths which more or less come into all traditionary lore, from passing
through ignorant mouths in the process of transmission.

Bridge of Alford

VIII.—ALFORD TO GLENBUCKET.

We'll awa', we'll awa' to the woods awa',
To the gorsy brae, and the birken shaw;
Where the hill burn rows, and the heather grows,
An' the bricht e'e o' heaven beams bonny owre a'.

WE are all familiar with the march between the Lowlands and the Highlands in Deeside, but where has that arbitrary line been fixed in Donside? It must certainly be West of the Vale of Alford; we should say in the gorge between Lord Arthur's Cairn and Coillebhar Hill. A parish boundary there suggests the entrance to the Highlands of the Don valley—the little Burn of Littlewood which separates Tullynessle-Forbes from Auchindoir-Kearn. The 30th milestone on the Aberdeen and Strathdon road stands hard by the crossing of this Burn, and thus the dividing line is definite and manifest. But the "Highland line" is considered by some authorities to have been advanced, in the latter days of cattle-lifting, to the neighbourhood of the church of Towie. It seems proper to mention here that so recently as 1766 school-masters were required to teach "Erse" as well as English in the "Highland parishes of the Presbytery [of Alford], Strathdon, &c".

At a Fountain in the village of Alford, erected as a memorial to the late proprietor of Haughton, the following distances are given :—

Miles.		Miles.	
1½	Bridge of Alford.	14⅞	Bridge of Bucket.
7½	Mossat.	18¾	Colquhonny.
9¾	Kildrummy Castle.	27¾	Cock Brig.
12	Bridge of Towie.		

It is from the 30th milestone that we really start on this stage of our journey, for during our stay in the Vale we have explored the district to that point. We may, however, recapitulate in a sentence or two the intervening miles and the more important objects by the way. We leave the village of Alford and the 25th milestone, pass on the right the road to Haughton and Montgarrie, traverse the battle-field, and pass the 26th milestone. At Cornerstonehouse, at the cross roads, a stone directs us on our journey, and so we hold Northwards, and are soon over the Bridge of Alford, whence we turn sharply to the left. Thereafter we pass the 27th, 28th and 29th milestones, and, a short distance to the left, Kirkton of Forbes, and, on the right, Littlewood Park, pleasantly situated on the

6

Southern slope of Lord Arthur's Cairn.   We enter now the
parish of Auchindoir-Kearn.

The principal estates, with their owners, in this parish are:
Clova, Hugh G. Lumsden; Druminnor, Trustees of the late
Robert Grant; Craig, William P. Craik;
Auchindoir-Kearn. Lordship of Forbes, Lord Forbes; and
Kildrummy, James Ogston. As the Bogie
drains the Northern part of the parish, we
need not go beyond Lumsden in our diversion from the
Strathdon road. The conjoined parish dates from 1811: Kearn
was at one time annexed to Forbes, but was disjoined about
1795.

The Don on our left is here rapid, rocky, and shallow;
Mossat Burn, which the road hugs for some distance, is some-
what sluggish in its upper course. Having passed, on the right,
Little Wood, surrounding Littlewood Park, we have Craigs of
Logie (1102 feet), a wooded height of Brux Hill (1558 feet), also on
the right. There is an interesting well on the South slope of
Craigs of Logie, North from the 31st milestone, at a height of
between 800 and 900 feet, known as Nine Maidens' Well. "The
Statistical Account", in referring to this Well, says: "near
which, tradition says, nine young women were slain by a boar
that infested the neighbouring country. A stone, with some
rude figures on it, marks the spot where this tragical event is
said to have happened. The boar was slain by a young man of
the name of Forbes, the lover of one of the young women, and
a stone with a boar's head cut on it, was set up to preserve the
remembrance of his gallantry and courage. The stone was
removed by Lord Forbes to his house at Putachie; and it is
from this circumstance that a boar's head is quartered in the
arms of that family". A variation of the tradition makes Forbes
exclaim, as he slew the animal, "It's a' *for-Bess*", Bess (or
Elizabeth) being the name of his sweetheart! The legend is
commemorated by "Boar Stone", a large flat stone on the roadside about 330 yards West from the Well. Still another version
may be given. The first of the name of Forbes was on the eve
of marriage with a beautiful heiress, who, accompanied by her
bridesmaids, went to a famed well to wash. The ladies were
attacked by a huge and ferocious wild boar, and the bride, with
some of her companions, was killed. The lover vowed revenge,
and made an end of the animal at the "Boar Stone", where it
was wont to sharpen its tusks. As he stabbed the brute he
exclaimed, at each thrust, "For Bess"—and so the name Forbes
is derived! The Forbes family got a footing in Kearn about
1330, the Gordons appearing in Auchindoir a little later.

The tradition of a bride washing at a well is by no means
uncommon. Farther up the valley there is a well, called
Bride's Well, which was long the resort of all the brides of the
district on the eve of their wedding. Accompanied only by
their "maidens" they paid their visit "atween the sun and the
sky", the maidens bathing the bride's feet and breasts. This

ensured that she should be no childless wife ; on leaving she dropped bread and cheese into the well, and her children were safe from want.

Lumsden (745 feet) is a little village between the watershed of the Don and that of the Bogie, about 9 miles from Alford and 8 from Gartly station. To the North, on one of the head-streams of the Water of Bogie, are Craig Castle and the Church of Auchindoir ; to the West, about a mile distant, is Clova, which is in the parish of Kildrummy. Clova House, built on the Eastern slope of Clova Hill (1611 feet), is a large mansion surrounded by extensive plantations. About three-quarters of a mile South from the house are the remains of the church (S. Luke's), of the ancient parish of Cloueth or Clova. The church of "Cloveth", with its lands was granted by Malcolm in 1063 to the church of S. Mary of Mortlach ; while in 1157 Pope Adrian IV. confirmed *the Monastery* to the Bishops of Aberdeen. In 1549 the Bishop leased the lands to Robert Lumisdane, probably an ancestor of the present lairds of Clova. The church and monas-tery stood on rising ground on the left bank of the Burn of Littlemill, a tributary of Mossat Burn. The site has been planted and enclosed ; the foundations show that the church had been about 31 feet long by 15 feet broad. The estate of New-mill bordered on the church property, but now forms part of Clova. Concerning one of the lairds it was said :—

> Here lies the Great Newmill,
> Wha liket aye the ither gill ;
> Aye ready wi' his aith and curse,
> But never cared to draw his purse.

Another of the Newmill lairds has a huge monument—Hill of John's Cairn (1745 feet), as on the O. S. map, but the old name was "John Reid's Cairn". At Chapeltown, close to Lumsden, where once an Episcopal Chapel stood, is the family mausoleum of Sir Harry Niven-Lumsden, Bart. of Auchindoir and Clova, who died in 1821.

Packet Burn, a tiny stream, flows on the West side of Lumsden to Mossat Burn. The site of the "Queen's Brig" which crossed it is still pointed out ; the name is derived from a tradition that Bruce's Queen, when hiding, took refuge there— a very improbable circumstance.

The Buck, which dominates so much of the upper part of the Don valley, has its summit at the meeting point of three parishes, Auchindoir-Kearn, Cabrach, and Kildrummy, and is frequently ascended from Lumsden. This hill, generally speaking, is of a soft, spongy, mossy formation ; viewed from the North-east its summit has a very elegant pyramidal shape, and is crowned by a large natural cairn, from which an extensive view of the country can be obtained. Looking across the Moray Firth the Caithness hills are seen under favourable weather conditions ; to the West, peak beyond peak of the Grampians. Lochnagar is one of the more particularly prominent mountains, and the Cairngorms are of course much in evidence.

Resuming our Westward journey, we return to the Strathdon road, and, crossing Mossat Burn, enter the parish of Kildrummy. The principal estates, with their owners, are : Kildrummy, James Ogston ; Clova, Hugh G. Lumsden ; Brux, Hon. Atholl M. Forbes ; and Glenkindie, Alexander H. Leith. The Duke of Fife holds the superiority of part of Kildrummy, as well as of most of the parish of Strathdon.

> Pleased with the calm bewitching hours,
> When evening shadows o'er the plain,
> I seek Kildrummy's roofless towers,
> And listen to the night owl's strain.
> Here where the verdant ash tree hangs,
> Once halls superb, majestic rose,
> Where chords with vibrating twangs
> High raised the soul, and cancelled woes.
> See here, where on the rugged ground,
> The mutilated fragments lie,
> Where erst arose the choral sound,
> And fuming incense floated high.

Both the parish and the castle of Kildrummy are of national interest, pre-historic as well as historic. Every mile of our journey has had its own particular "human **Kildrummy.** interest" ; here we reach the culminating point. "The castle, one of the largest in Scotland, is itself, indeed, the most truly picturesque object in the whole Strath". The history of the ancient territorial Earldom of Mar is, as stated by Lord Hailes, "lost in the mists of antiquity". The Earldom consisted of the whole of the upper and Western parts of Aberdeenshire, and was at one time held along with the Earldom of Garioch. Previous to the 15th century, large tracts of the lands of the old Earldom had been alienated, and portions had been frequently given to provide dowries for relatives of those in possession of the Earldom— ("Story of a Donside Estate", by Colonel James Allardyce, LL.D.)

Even in pre-historic times, Kildrummy had been a considerable settlement ; it may well be compared to Dinnet on Deeside. An extraordinary number of Eirde Houses have been discovered in various parts of the parish ; between Drumnahive Wood and Mossat Burn, there are no fewer than ten within a space about three quarters of a mile long, by half a mile broad. Flint arrowheads have also been found in considerable numbers, as well as bronze celts, querns, stone ladles, axes, and coffins. In Burton's "History of Scotland" the following reference is made to Eirde Houses :—

"Another class of structures very abundant in Scotland are called Eard or Earth-house, Picts'-houses and Weems . . . They exist in many places in Scotland, but chiefly they concentrate themseves near Glenkindy and Kildrummy, on the upper reaches of the Don. There they may be found so thickly strewn as to form subterranean villages, or even towns. The fields are, to use a common expression, honey-combed with them. They give no artificial signs above ground. The peasant will sometimes know where they are by an unploughed patch in the field, in which a few stones crop above ground, with furze growing between them ; in other instances the earth above is sufficient to let the plough pass over the edifice, and a small hole between two projecting stones marks its entrance. Through this hole a corpulent man will find difficulty in squeezing himself. It brings him to a sloping tunnel, which he descends some six or eight feet. He is then in a subterranean gallery, in which he may be able to stand upright ; the ordinary height varies from five to eight feet. It is some thirty feet long, and may probably have lateral galleries to the right and the left. There are few places in which the sensation of the dungeon or burial in life is stronger than in those artificial caverns, and that on account of the colossal and massive character of the roof. There is no cement, and no mark of tooling on the stones. If the gallery be eight feet broad at the floor, which is not an uncommon breadth, the walls, built of rough stones, will be found so to slope inwards by overlapping as to bring the sides within six feet of each other. Across this breadth are laid gigantic blocks of granite " [or other stone].

The Strathdon road makes a great diversion from the river between Invermossat and Kildrummy church– taking the North instead of the South side of the hill (1082 feet) of Ardhuncart Wood. The river has one of its numerous crooks at Invermossat, where it forms (on the right bank) Machar's Haugh. " The Corbies", the North-western point of Coillebhar Hill, rises over 500 feet on the South side of the Haugh ; and presents not a few interesting spots in connection with the old estate of Brux. The supposed site of S. Machar's Chapel is at the South end of the Haugh ; Chapel Haugh and Chapel Ford across the Don indicate the existence of an old place of worship. Jonathan Forbes, the laird of Brux, was " out " in the '45, and took part in the battle of Culloden. He was more successful in eluding the military who were sent in search of him than his fellow officer of Terpersie. He for a time betook himself to building stone dykes on his own estate—some of which were substantial enough, it is said, to remain to this day—the better to escape detection. He had two caves on " The Corbies", one on the North, the other on the South side of the summit, where he retired as circumstances dictated. A party of soldiers approached him as he was " dykeing " one forenoon, and asked him if the laird was at home. The reply was, " Yes, he was in the house when I was at breakfast ". On this he was left alone, only to betake himself to one of his caves in case the search should become too hot. Possibly profiting from his building operations, in quieter times he is said to have erected with his own hands his tomb in the Howff Park between the Mains of Brux and " The Corbies". He died in bed—instead of at Carlisle as did Terpersie,—about 1802, and was interred in the Howff alongside his mother. The old lady is said to have protested against her son's proposal to bury her on the wrong side of the Don, on unconsecrated ground, but he, having turned Quaker, would only undertake to carry her body to the churchyard should it fail to find rest in the place of his selection. But there are numerous forms of such grave traditions.

There is an interesting tradition connecting the Mowats, proprietors of Abergeldie, and the Camerons of Brux, between which families there had long existed a deadly feud. At last it was agreed between the two lairds that an end should be made of the struggle for supremacy by a meeting with each other on the hill (1162 feet) now known as Drumgoudrum Wood, each laird to be accompanied by eleven horsemen. The two parties met as arranged, but the wily Mowat had a foot-soldier mounted behind each horseman. The Donside men, however, bravely faced their treacherous opponents, but the unequal contest made an end of the male line of the Camerons of Brux. Cameron's Hillock on the South-west side of the hill, is a suggestive name ; near by is McFadyen's Well, close to which the Abergeldie men who fell in the contest were said to have been buried.

The laird of Brux left an only daughter, Catherine, too good a prize to lack admirers, who at once declared that her hand and all that went with it should reward the man bold enough to kill the laird of Abergeldie. The challenge was at once accepted by Alexander Forbes, a son of Lord Forbes, and a combat between his clansmen and the Mowats was agreed upon at Badaneoin. Both arrived in Glen Bucket with an equal number of followers, when to prevent useless bloodshed Forbes proposed a single combat between the leaders. Mowat agreed, with the result that he was killed by his young opponent, and buried under a great cairn, Clochmowat, or Mowat's Stone. Forbes married the heiress, and thus founded the family of Forbes of Brux.

The church of Kildrummy is near the 34th mile-stone, between the road and the river, North-west from Drumgoudrum Wood. It is said it was once called the " Chappel of the Lochs ", from having been surrounded on all sides by a marsh. The style of the present building is fortunately becoming exceedingly rare. The only remains of its predecessor, which was dedicated to S. Bride, are parts of the North and East walls and the Elphinstone burial place, which formed the South aisle. The surname Elphinstone, probably from an estate of the name near Edinburgh, first appeared in 1250 ; Alexander, who fell at Flodden, was the first of the family to hold lands on Donside. The tomb fell into disrepair after the Elphinstones left Kildrummy, but, as an inscription bears, it was " Restored by William, 15th Lord Elphinstone, 1862 ", after a pilgrimage to the lands and burial aisle of his forefathers—as told in " Jervise ".

A flat stone is inscribed to " Michael Dunbar, who died Decr. the 9, 1722, and of age 100 years ". There is a peculiar tradition concerning this centenarian, which has been found to be without foundation :—Dunbar was wont to feign feebleness of body as he hung about in search of his prey. His time came when a passing stranger happened to ask him the road to Kildrummy Castle. Be the stranger mounted or on foot he was soon despatched by the robber's dirk. When a day passed without

Kildrummy Castle

a victim he considered that he had lost a day. Now for the facts. In Dunbar's time his native parish, Kildrummy, was particularly subject to forays by Highland caterans. The inhabitants naturally combined together for defence, and Dunbar, who had great bodily strength and daring, combined with skill, was appointed their leader. There was rough work to be done, and somebody had to do it. On his deathbed he was told by the Rev. William Miln, the minister of Kildrummy, that he must repent of his sins, alluding particularly to the fact that Michael now and again helped himself to more cattle from the cateran than had been "lifted" from Kildrummy. These animals, he was told, would stand against him on the day of judgment; "Weel, weel, then," replied Michael, "ilka chiel will get his ain then. But here's the dirk that lat oot the bleed o' fifteen caterans in ae nicht. Surely that will shorten her stay in Purgatory"!

> The drawbridge pois'd or clanking chain,
>   Descends no more at peep of morn
> To usher forth the noble train,
>   With prancing steed and echoing horn.
> The bridge is fall'n : the moat is dry ;
>   The portal arch returns no sound,
> Or echoes but the raven's cry,
>   That rings the mouldering turrets round.
> Nameless am I, and landless all,
>   Yet have I gazed on thee with tears,
> Whose mossy walls and towers recall
>   The memory of a thousand years.

Kildrummy Castle stands on the wayside, close to the 35th milestone, between two "dens"—The Den of Kildrummy on the South-east and Back Den on the North-west. The position had doubtless been carefully selected, for the natural conformation of the ground rendered it somewhat difficult of access. The date of the oldest portion is probably 1172. It was the stronghold of the old royal domain of the Garioch, and the appanage of David, Earl of Huntingdon, brother of William the Lion. It thus fell to the Bruce, and thereafter passed by his sister's marriage to the Earls of Mar. The castle had not only been of great extent, but of much architectural importance as well as strength of masonry. Built of freestone, the outer blocks are as regularly squared and as closely jointed as the finest of modern erections. In spite of the original thickness of the masonry there is not a single wall left entire ; the outer walls were generally about nine feet in breadth, the interior about four feet. Soon after the forfeiture of the Mar estates the castle was partly demolished by the Royalist party, and its ruins were locally regarded as at the disposal of any one who had byre or barn to build. The finest fragment still standing is the Eastern gable with three lancet windows of the chapel ; "almost all that remains on which the eye can rest with pleasure ; ghastly looking masses of stone and rubbish being nearly all that now exist of the once splendid fabric".

The Snow Tower, the erection of which was commenced in 1172, is believed to have been the nucleus of the group of buildings of various dates which formed the royal castle. This tower, which received its name from the colour of the stone with which it was built, consisted, it is said, of five storeys, and was the most important part of the building. "Through this passed a massy chain, suspended at the top, and reaching to the ground for the more commodiously raising water for the use of the upper apartments. Some old men who remember when the chain was taken away, say that there was a deep well underneath".—(Cordiner's "Antiquities and Scenery of the North of Scotland", 1776.) The great hall, which was on the North-west side, can still be traced. It measured 73 feet by 40; the chapel also, 35 feet by 20, is distinctly indicated.

Edward I. visited the castle in 1296, and received homage there; in 1298 Sir William Wallace is believed to have spent several days in it. After The Bruce's defeat at the battle of Methven he retreated North, and his Queen, with several members of his household, found shelter for a time in Kildrummy. Edward sent an army in 1307 to lay siege to the castle, a siege which is the most famous episode in its history. The besiegers, other means failing, at last captured the castle by burning it. According to tradition the local blacksmith agreed to betray the castle, and so set fire to the hay-loft with a red-hot bar. As he had covenanted for as much gold as he could carry, the precious metal was *poured* hot down his throat. It was, however, rebuilt soon after, for it stood another siege—this time by the Earl of Athole—in 1335. He had to retire rather precipitately to Deeside, where his forces were defeated at Culblean.

David II. made some stay in Kildrummy in 1342, and in 1361 the king besieged and captured the castle owing to a quarrel with the Earl of Mar. The Earl, however, had it restored to him eventually, and was buried within the walls. In 1403 Sir Malcolm Drummond, the husband of the Countess of Mar, was attacked and killed in the castle, Alexander Stewart, a natural son of the Wolf of Badenoch, being generally regarded as responsible for the outrage. At all events, he successfully stormed the castle shortly after the murder of Drummond, and by fair means or foul married the recently widowed Countess, and procured from her a charter in his own favour.

The outrage thus committed (says the Earl of Crawford and Balcarres in "The Earldom of Mar") on Isabel's person and property, and the extortion of the charter, were too flagrant in themselves, and affected too many contingent interests, to remain unredressed. On the other hand, Alexander's connection with the royal family, together with his father's great power, and the paralysis of law in those northern regions, may have secured him from actual punishment. The result was that a compromise was arranged, by which the rights of all the parties concerned were secured, and under which Isabel *appears* to have been willing to condone the violence of her rough wooer.

In implement of this arrangement Isabel agreed to execute a new charter in favour of Stewart, to the same general effect as the former one, granting him the Earldoms of Mar and Garioch, and other possessions, under contract of marriage, but with reservation of liferent enjoyment to the longest liver, and ultimate destination to her heirs in case of their being no issue from the marriage. But before executing this charter, it was considered necessary, in Isabel's interest, that the wrong previously done should be publicly redressed, and Isabel replaced in her free rights and exercise of free agency by the actual hand which had despoiled her of them. Everything in these days was done with picturesque ceremonial. Isabel accordingly, on 9th September, 1404, accompanied by Alexander, Bishop of Ross, and several gentlemen of the district, and attended by a large concourse of people, took up her station on a meadow outside the great gate of the castle, and stood there, conversing familiarly with the Bishop and others. Stewart then came forth of the gate, and advanced to where she stood ; and, in the presence of all assembled, as described in a legal document drawn up on the occasion, delivered over to her the castle, with its charters and evidents, the silver vessels and other jewels, and everything therein, placing the keys in her hands in symbol of the transfer, to dispose of the whole—and her person as no longer under constraint—at her free and uncontrolled pleasure. This having been done, Isabel, holding the keys in her hands as châtelaine, made choice of Stewart as her husband before all the people, and gave him in free marriage the castle, the Earldoms of Mar and Garioch, and all that she possessed.

Stewart died without heirs male, so James II., in violation of the rights of Sir Robert Erskine, the undoubted heir of the Countess Isabel, created his own son Earl of Mar ; but as the new Earl left no heirs James III. bestowed the Earldom on Robert Cochrane, one of his favourites, who came to an untimely end. On 19th July, 1508, James IV. granted a charter to his "intimate friends, Alexander Elphinstone of Invernochty and his wife, Elizabeth Berlay", conferring upon them the Mains of Kildrummy and other lands, the whole being incorporated into a Barony and called the Barony of Invernochty, carrying with it the custody of the Castle of Kildrummy". In the following year Alexander Elphinstone was created Lord Elphinstone and these lands were formed "into a free Barony, to be called the Barony of Kildrummy in all time coming". Ultimately Queen Mary, recognising the claim of the Erskines, conferred the title and estates on that family. Following on a decision of the Court of Session the Mar family, on taking over the Barony, paid according to an amicable arrangement 48,000 merks to the Elphinstones for ameliorations. It was not till 1626 that the Court of Session reduced the charter dated 1508, while the decrees in the various actions of removings that ensued against Lord Elphinstone and his tenants or vassals were not pronounced till 1635. Thereafter Kildrummy bulked little in the affairs of the nation. The Mar estates were forfeited in 1716, and a few years afterwards Kildrummy was purchased by Gordon of Wardhouse, in whose family it remained till its recent acquisition by the present proprietor. That gentleman is anxious to prevent further destruction to the castle. Some visitors carve their names or initials on the walls, others even add to the ruins. In common with him we ask the assistance of the public in preserving as much as possible one of the grandest monuments which Scotland boasts.

A curious discovery was made in 1746 in the vault where the Mar family are said to have been laid under the aisle of Kildrummy church, the embalmed body of a lady being found in a perfect state of preservation. It was believed to have been that of the wife of Gratney, Earl of Mar, or of Isabel, Countess of Mar, who married Alexander Stewart.

The following letter, dated 8th May, 1607, was written by James I. to the Earl of Mar : " Dear Jock. As I'm gaing to gie an audience this morning to the French Ambassador, I deseir you to be sae gude to send me a pair of yeir best silken hose, with the goud clocks at them. Your affectionate Cusine, JAMES R ".

The new house of Kildrummy stands on the opposite side of Back Den facing the castle.

> Here stop and weep o'er Towie's roofless towers,
> Where loyal Forbes spent his youthful hours.
> But silence reigns ; no bard extempore sings,
> Nor maiden minstrel shakes the sounding strings.
> Each vaulted arch to whistling winds responds
> With hollow murmurs and with dismal sounds.

Kildrummy Castle is on the borders of Towie, the Den of Kildrummy being the march on the South-east ; Glaschul Hill (1177 feet) stands between it and the Don.

Towie. The principal estates in Towie, with their owners, are : Towie, Hugh G. Lumsden, and James Ogston ; Glenkindie, Alexander H. Leith ; Colquoich, Colonel James Allardyce, LL.D. ; and Brux, Hon. Atholl M. Forbes. The Glenkindie Arms Inn is near the 37th milestone, opposite which, on the South side of the river, are the church and the ruined castle of Towie ; Glenkindie House, near Inverkindie, is between the 38th and 39th milestones. Colquoich is on the right bank of the Don, opposite the 39th milestone.

As shewing the old close relations between Kildrummy and Towie it may be mentioned that the Earl of Mar and Sir Thomas Craig, the governor of Kildrummy Castle, are said to have built the Church of Towie in 1385, in order to commemorate the successful defence of the castle fifty years previously. Cairn Fichlie, on Glaschul Hill, is also a memorial of the defeat of Athole's forces. The Peel of Fichlie is between that hill and the river. The Peel is a mound surrounded by a fosse ; the height is about 60 feet, and

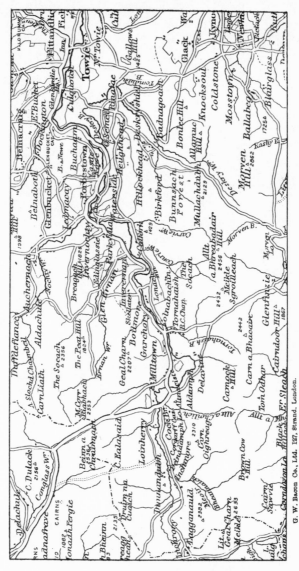

W. JOLLY & SONS, PUBLISHERS, ABERDEEN.

Face p. 98.

G. W. Bacon & Co., Ltd. 127, Strand, London.

the breadth, at the summit, on which are some vitrified remains, 200 feet by 127. The district, like Kildrummy, had been early peopled ; Eirde Houses and other indications of antiquity are numerous. At Sinnahard, on the right bank of the river, opposite the Peel of Fichlie, is Chapelton, the name being derived from the site there of an old chapel and graveyard. There is another chapel site at Nether Towie on the left bank of Burn of Towie ; and one at Belnaboth, fully half a mile to the West of the castle. Chapels also existed, it is said, at Kinbattoch (which had evidently been fortified), about a mile South-west from the castle, and at Ley, between Glaschul Hill and the Don.

The church is on the right bank of the Don, near the confluence of the Burn of Towie ; the burial aisle of Lumsden of Corrachree adjoins the site of the previous building. Hard by is a fragment of a square tower, with a vaulted cellar—all that remains of Towie Castle.

> And on thy bleak and ruin'd wa's
> Nae banners now are streaming ;
> The bat and jay flit through thy ha's,
> And night owls there are screaming.

The Forbeses of Towie are said to have been descended from Alexander Forbes of Brux, who died in 1494. Towie remained in their possession for nearly two centuries. The date of the commencement of the building of the castle is not known ; it has been a ruin since 1571, when it was burned (according to some authorities) by Captain Ker, acting under the orders of Sir Edom (Adam) Gordon of Auchendown, a brother of the Marquis of Huntly. The laird, Alexander Forbes, was absent, and his wife bravely declined to surrender in response to Ker's summons that the castle should "be randrit to him in the Queynis name". But "fyre was put to the hous, wharin she, and the nomber of 27 persons, war cruelie brynt to the death".

"Don" states that the castle was never finished : "it had all its lower flat arched, and one end of four storeys slated ; it broke three lairds in rearing up what now remains ; and the three different kinds of work are visible to this day". Even the surrounding dyke is in a ruinous condition.

Glenkindie House has a charming situation, on the left bank of the Don, near Kindy Burn. The plantations consist of old ash, elm, sycamore and birch, with some particularly fine spruces, as well as other varieties of trees. The present house, which is ivy-clad, replaces one which, built by the Strachans in 1595, had stood near by. "Replaced" is now (1900) the proper expression ; for it, with the exception of two old wings, has been pulled down, and a large and palatial mansion is in the course of erection. A short distance to the West there are the remains of a fort with a fosse. The old house of the Strachans was plundered in 1639 by Farquharson of Monaltrie, and demolished in 1644. About two miles up the glen, near the junction of

Chapel Burn and Kindy Burn, are the remains of a chapel dedicated to S. Ronald. The estate of Culquoich takes its name from the formation of the ground. About the middle of the property there is a cup-shaped hollow (quoich) at the corner or back of the hill (cul). The old house of Culquoich stood amongst some fine old trees a little to the West of the present house. It had been the residence of the Elphinstones of Culquoich and Barns, descended from a second son of one of the Lords Elphinstone who got Kildrummy as above stated. After the time of the Elphinstones it was occupied by the Inneses of Culquoich. Clachcurr Hill (1379 feet) stands within a loop of the river, its name meaning the hill by the Stone Seat, or Stone Chair. There was a rock by the side of the Don, immediately West of this hill, which was called the Laird's Seat, or Laird's Chair. It was removed to make room for the turnpike road.— ("Story of a Donside Estate".)

The parish of Glenbucket is entered a little to the East of Bridge of Bucket (799 feet) ; its breadth, along the Don, is under one mile, but the length, along the Water of **Glenbucket.** Bucket, is about seven miles. The Gordons were long the proprietors of the glen ; the last laird of that name was an accomplished man, who fought for the Stewarts in both the '15 and the '45. Though an old man, he was present at the head of his regiment at Culloden, after which he escaped to France, where he died at a very advanced age. He was a personal friend of the Prince, and thus shared his exile. His name was a power in itself, and it is even said that George II. was troubled in his dreams by it ! Glenbucket Castle, which stands on the right bank of the Bucket near its confluence with the Don at Bridge of Bucket, was built in 1590, and is a fine specimen of a baron's residence of that time. It is admirably situated on the Eastern slope of Ben Newe (1855 feet), over-looking the valley, and the ruins are still viewed with interest, both on their own account, and from their association with chivalrous "old Glenbucket". Architectural experts consider the castle a fine specimen of the class having square towers at diagonally opposite angles ; its substantial masonry has defied time. The estate was purchased in 1738 by the Earl of Fife ; the Duke of Fife sold it to the late Mr. Henry Burra. Over the castle doorway is engraved : NOCHT . ON . EARTH . REMAINS . BOT . FAME. Strong as are his castle walls the "Fame" of its last occupant will outlast them.

The glen, which is synonymous with the estate and the parish, is hilly ; the lowest part on the Don is at an altitude of 774 feet ; the church stands at 1070 feet. On the North-west the parish borders with Banffshire on the Deveron and the Avon water-sheds. The Water of Bucket is formed by the junction of two burns which meet below Badaneoin—the Westerly, Coulins Burn, rises on Geal Charn (2241 feet), the Easterly, Leadensider Burn, in a small tarn (1823 feet) near the summit of Crespet Hill. There is a shooting box, Glenbucket

Glenbucket Castle

Lodge, on the left bank of Coulins Burn, near Backies; at Badaneoin is the site of the castle of that name. Badaneoin Castle was, according to tradition, built by one of the Mowats (see page 94) in the thirteenth century. John of Badaneoin has been rendered famous by a ballad by Rev. John Skinner. Mowat's Stone stood between Glenbucket Lodge and Badaneoin; it was, alas, broken up by a mason for building purposes. We have referred more than once, in other pages than these, to Alexander Davidson, the last of the old Deeside poachers. He was found dead on Creag an Sgor, in Glen Bucket, on 25th August, 1843; a cairn, near the peat road, marks the spot. His body was interred in the churchyard of Glenmuick.

The summit of Ben Newe is only about three-quarters of a mile from the church, and a mile from the castle of Glenbucket, from either of which the ascent is an easy matter. The hill is a prominent object in the strath, not only from its height, but also from the "shaved" appearance of the upper part. The view is extensive—The Buck, Bennachie, the Deeside hills, and the Cairngorms may be named; while the nearer brown and tawny hills are relieved by green valleys; between them the Don is seen above Pooldhulie and below Bridge of Bucket.

GLENLOGIE.

1. There were four-and-twenty ladies dined i the Queen's ha,
    And Jean o Bethelnie was the flower o' them a'.

2. Four-and-twenty gentlemen rode thro Banchory fair,
    But bonny Glenlogie was the flower that was there.

3. Young Jean at a window she chanced to sit nigh,
    And upon Glenlogie she fixed an eye.

4. She called on his best man, unto him did say,
    O what is that knight's name? or where does he stay?

5. 'He's of the noble Gordons, of great birth and fame;
    He stays at Glenlogie, Sir George is his name.'

6. Then she wrote a broad letter, and wrote it in haste;
    To send to Glenlogie, she thought it was best.

7. Says, O brave Glenlogie, unto me be kind;
    I've laid my love on you, and told you my mind.

8. Then reading the letter, as he stood on the green.
    Says, I leave you to judge, sirs; what does women mean?

9. Then turned about sprightly, as the Gordons do a';
    'Lay not your love on me, I'm promised awa.'

10. When she heard this answer, her heart was like to break,
    That she laid her love on him, and him so ungrate.

11. Then she called on her maidens to lay her to bed.
    And take her fine jewels and lay them aside.

12.   'My seals and my signets, no more shall I crave ;
      But linen and trappin, a chest and a grave.'

13.   Her father stood by her, possessëd with fear,
      To see his poor daughter possessëd with care.

14.   Says, Hold your tongue, Jeannie, let all your folly be ;
      I'll wed you to Dumfedline, he is better than he.

15.   'O hold your tongue, father, and let me alane,
      If I getna Glenlogie, I'll never have ane.

16.   'His bonny jimp middle, his black rolling eye,
      If I getna Glenlogie, I'm sure I shall die.'

17.   But her father's old chaplain, a man of great skill,
      He wrote a broad letter, and pennëd it well.

18.   Saying, O brave Glenlogie, why must it be so ?
      A maid's love laid on you, shall she die in her woe ?

19.   Then reading the letter, his heart was like to break
      That such a leal virgin should die for his sake.

20.   Then he called on his footman, and likewise his groom,
      Says, Get my horse saddled and bridlëd soon.

21   Before the horse was saddled and brought to the yate,
      Bonnie Glenlogie was five miles on foot.

22.   When he came to Bethelnie, he saw nothing there
      But weeping and wailing, vexation and care.

23.   Then out spake her father, with the tear in his ee,
      You're welcome, Glenlogie, you're welcome to me.

24.   'If ye make me welcome, as welcome's ye say,
      Ye'll show me the chamber where Jeannie does lay.'

25.   Then one of the maidens took him by the hand,
      To show him the chamber where Jeannie lay in.

26.   Before that she saw him, she was pale and wan :
      But when she did see him she grew ruddy again.

27.   'O turn bonny Jeannie, turn to your side ;
      For I'll be the bridegroom, and ye'll be the bride.'

28.   When Jeannie was married, her tocher down tauld,
      Bonnie Jean o' Bethelnie was fifteen years auld.*

---

* The above is Buchan's text, " Ballads of the North of Scotland,"¡I. p. 188.—Nine
versions are given by Professor Child—the earliest of which, dated April, 1768, is
among the Percy Papers, and was communicated to Percy by Robert Lambe of
Norham, August, 1768. In it the hero is " Earl Ogie," and the story is identical
with that printed above, while the others are all more or less fragmentary. The
names of persons and places vary—" Earl Ogie," " Glenogie," " Glenlogie ; "—
" Bethelnie," " Belhelvie."   If what Buchan says in his note to the ballad were
correct, the maiden's name must have been Seaton, and not Melville—the Seatons
and Urquharts being the only two names which in historical times could be called
lairds of Meldrum or Bethelnie.   A late tradition on Donside associated the hero of
the ballad with the Gordons of Glenbucket. Glenlogie lies in the parish of Auchindoir,
about five miles West from the village of Alford.—Music : " Smith Scottish Minstrel,"
IV. p. 78 ; " Christie's Ballad Airs," I. p. 54.

THE EARL OF MAR'S DAUGHTER.

1. It was intill a pleasant time,
   Upon a simmer's day,
   The noble Earl of Mar's daughter
   Went forth to sport and play.

2. As thus she did amuse hersell,
   Below a green aik tree,
   There she saw a sprightly doo
   Set on a tower sae hie.

3. ' O Cow-me-doo, my love sae true,
   If ye'll come down to me,
   Ye'se hae a cage o' guid red gowd
   Instead o simple tree :

4. ' I'll put gowd hinges roun your cage,
   And siller roun your wa ;
   I'll gar ye shine as fair a bird
   As ony o them a'.'

5. But she hadna these words well spoke,
   Nor yet these words well said,
   Till Cow-me-doo flew frae the tower
   And lighted on her head.

6. Then she has brought this pretty bird
   Hame to her bowers and ha,
   And made him shine as fair a bird
   As ony o them a'.

7. When day was gane, and night was come,
   About the evening tide,
   This lady spied a sprightly youth
   Stand straight up by her side.

8. ' From whence came ye, young man ? ' she said ;
   That does surprise me sair ;
   My door was bolted right secure,
   What way hae ye come here ? '

9. O had your tongue, ye lady fair,
   Lat a' your folly be ;
   Mind ye not on your turtle-doo
   Last day ye brought wi thee ? '

10. ' O tell me mair, young man ', she said,
    ' This does surprise me now ;
    What country hae ye come frae ?
    What pedigree are you ? '

11. ' My mither lives on foreign isles,
    She has nae mair but me ;
    She is a queen o wealth and state,
    And birth and high degree.

12. ' Likewise well skilld in magic spells,
     As ye may plainly see.
   And she tranformed me to yon shape,
     To charm such maids as thee.

13. ' I am a doo the live-lang day,
     A sprightly youth at night ;
   This aye gars me appear mair fair
     In a fair maiden's sight.

14. ' And it was but this verra day
     That I came ower the sea ;
   Your lovely face did me enchant ;
     I'll live and dee wi thee.'

15. ' O Cow-me-doo, my luve sae true,
     Nae mair frae me ye'se gae ; '
   ' That's never my intent, my luve,
     As ye said, it shall be sae.'

16. ' O Cow-me-doo, my luve sae true,
     It's time to gae to bed ; '
   ' Wi' a my heart, my dear marrow,
     It's be as ye hae said.'

17. Then he has staid in bower wi her
     For sax lang years and ane,
   Till sax young sons to him she bare,
     And the seventh she's brought hame.

18. But aye as ever a child was born
     He carried them away,
   And brought them to his mither's care,
     As fast as he coud fly.

19. Thus he had staid in bower wi her
     For twenty years and three ;
   There came a lord o high renown
     To court this fair ladie.

20. But still his proffer she refused,
     And a' his presents too ;
   Says, I'm content to live alane
     Wi my bird, Cow-me-doo.

21. Her father sware a solemn oath
     Amang the nobles all,
   ' The morn, or ere I eat or drink,
     This bird I will gar kill.'

22. The bird was sitting in his cage,
     And heard what they did say ;
   And when he found they were dismist,
     Says, ' Wae's me for this day ! '

23. ' Before that I da longer stay,
    And thus to be forlorn,
I'll gang unto my mither's bower,
    Where I was bred and born.'

24. Then Cow-me-doo took flight and flew
    Beyond the raging sea,
And lighted near his mither's castle,
    On a tower o gowd sae hie.

25. As his mither was wauking out,
    To see what she coud see,
And there she saw her little son,
    Set on the tower sae hie.

26. ' Get dancers here to dance,' she said,
    ' And minstrells for to play ;
For here's my young son, Florentine,
    Come here wi' me to stay.'

27. ' Get nae dancers to dance, mither,
    Nor minstrells for to play,
For the mither o my seven sons,
    The morn's her wedding-day.'

28. ' O tell me, tell me Florentine,
    Tell me, and tell me true,
Tell me this day without a flaw,
    What I will do for you.'

29. ' Instead o dancers to dance, mither,
    Or minstrells for to play,
Turn four-and-twenty wall-wight men,
    Like storks in feathers grey ;

30. ' My seven sons in seven swans,
    Aboon their heads to flee ;
And I mysell a gay gos-hawk,
    A bird o high degree.'

31. Then sichin said the queen hersell,
    ' That things too high for me ; '
But she applied to an auld woman,
    Who had mair skill than she.

32. Instead o dancers to dance a dance,
    Or minstrells for to play,
Four-and-twenty wall-wight men,
    Turned birds o feathers grey.

33. Her seven sons in seven swans,
    Aboon their heads to flee ;
And he himsell a gay gos-hawk,
    A bird o high degree.

7

34. This flock o birds took flight and flew
        Beyond the raging sea,
    And landed near the Earl Mar's castle,
        Took shelter in every tree.

35. They were a flock o pretty birds,
        Right comely to be seen ;
    The people viewed them wi surprise,
        As they dancd on the green.

36. These birds ascended frae the tree,
        And lighted on the ha,
    And at the last wi force did flee
        Amang the nobles a'.

37. The storks there seized some o the men,
        They coud neither fight nor flee ;
    The swans they bound the bride's best man,
        Below a green aik tree.

38. They lighted next on maidens fair,
        Then on the bride's own head,
    And wi the twinkling o an ee,
        The bride and them were fled.

39. There's ancient men at weddings been
        For sixty years or more,
    But sic a curious wedding-day
        They never saw before.

40. For naething coud the companie do,
        Nor naething coud they say
    But they saw a flock o pretty birds
        That took their bride away.*

CAPTAIN CAR, OR EDOM O GORDON.

1. It fell about the Martinmas,
        When the wind blew schrile and cauld,
    Said Edom o Gordon to his men,
        We maun draw to a hald.

2. 'And what an a hald sall we draw to,
        My merry men and me ?
    We will gae to the house of [Towie],
        To see that fair lady.'

*This is from Buchan's "Ballads of the North of Scotland," I. p. 49. No other
copy has been recovered from tradition, and Buchan neither in his printed notes nor
manuscript collections gives any clue to where he found it. Though Professor Child
points out elements of remote kinship to the story in Danish, Scandinavian, and other
ballads, he has no hesitation in saying that it has no claim either to age or vogue.
There is in it the same needless spinning out by repetitions which characterises the
ignorant singers and reciters of Buchan's time, and is probably another of the many
doubtful contributions which "Jamie Rankin," that "wight o' Homer's craft," was
wont to supply to the too eager collector. We have omitted the last verse—so
palpably absurd and modern.—Music in "Christie's Ballad Airs" II. p. 38.

3. She had nae sooner busket her sell,
   Nor putten on her gown,
   Till Edom o Gordon and his men
   Were round about the town.

4. They had nae sooner sitten down,
   Nor sooner said the grace,
   Till Edom o Gordon and his men
   Were closed about the place.

5. The lady ran up to her towe-head,
   As fast as she could drie,
   To see if by her fair speeches
   She could with him agree.

6. As soon he saw the lady fair,
   And her yates all locked fast,
   He fell into a rage of wrath,
   And his heart was aghast.

7. 'Cum down to me, ye lady fair,
   Cum down to me ; let's see ;
   This night ye's ly by my ain side,
   The morn my bride sall be.'

8. 'I winnae cum down, ye fals Gordon,
   I winnae cum down to thee ;
   I winnae forsake my ain dear lord,
   That is sae far frae me.'

9. 'Gi up your house, ye fair lady,
   Gi up your house to me,
   Or I will burn yoursel therein,
   Bot and your babies three."

10. 'I winnae gie up, you fals Gordon,
    To nae sik traitor as thee,
    Tho you should burn mysel therein,
    Bot and my babies three."

11. 'Set fire to the house,' quoth fals Gordon,
    'Sin better may nae bee ;
    And I will burn hersel therein,
    Bot and her babies three.'

12. 'And ein wae worth ye, Jock my man !
    I paid ye weil your fee ;
    Why pow ye out my ground-wa-stane,
    Lets in the reek to me?

13. 'And ein wae worth ye, Jock my man !
    For I paid ye weil your hire ;
    Why pow ye out my ground-wa-stane,
    To me lets in the fire ?'

14. 'Ye paid me weil my hire, lady,
    Ye paid me weil my fee,
    But now I'm Edom o Gordon's man,
    Maun either do or die.'

15. O then bespake her youngest son,
      Sat on the nurses knee,
    ' Dear mother, gie owre your house,' he says,
      ' For the reek it worries me.'

16. ' I winnae gie up my house, my dear,
      To nae sik traitor as he ;
    Cum weil, cum wae, my jewels fair,
      Ye maun tak share wi me.'

17. O then bespake her dochter dear,
      She was baith jimp and sma ;
    ' O row me in a pair o shiets,
      And tow me owre the wa.'

18. They rowd her in a pair o shiets,
      And towd her owre the wa,
    But on the point of Edom's speir
      She gat a deadly fa.

19. O bonny, bonny was her mouth,
      And chirry were her cheiks,
    And clear, clear was hir yellow hair,
      Whereon the reid bluid dreips !

20. Then wi his speir he turned her owr ;
      O gin hir face was wan !
    He said, You are the first that eer
      I wist alive again.

21. He turned hir owr and owr again ;
      O gin her skin was white !
    He said, I might ha spard thy life
      To been some man's delyte.

22. ' Busk and boon, my merry men all,
      For ill dooms I do guess ;
    I cannae luik in that bonny face,
      As it lyes on the grass.'

23. ' Them luiks to freits, my master deir,
      Then freits will follow them ;
    Let it neir be said brave Edom o' Gordon
      Was daunted with a dame.'

24. O then he spied hir ain deir lord,
      As he cam owr the lee ;
    He saw his castle in a fire
      As far as he could see.

25. ' Put on, put on, my mighty men,
      As fast as ye can drie !
    For he that's hindmost of my men
      Sall neir get guid o' me.'

26. And some they raid, and some they ran,
      Fu fast out-owr the plain,
    But lang, lang eer he could get up
      They were a' deid and slain.

27. But mony were the mudie men
    Lay gasping on the grien,
    For o' fifty men that Edom brought out
    There were but five ged heme.

28. And mony were the mudie men
    Lay gasping on the grien,
    And mony were the fair ladys
    Lay lemanless at heme.

29. And round and round the waes he went,
    Their ashes for to view ;
    At last into the flames he flew,
    And bade the world adieu.*

* The above is the first printed version of Edom o Gordon, issued by R. and A. Foulis, Glasgow, 1755, taken from a copy supplied by Sir David Dalrymple " who gave it as preserved in the memory of a lady." Two earlier texts are printed in Child's " English and Scottish Popular Ballads," but they are English versions, one contained in a manuscript in the British Museum, written very shortly after the event [about 1580], the other contained in the Percy folio MS. [about 1650]. Every copy recorded by Professor Child gives a different locality as the scene of the tragic event. When Percy published the text given above in his " Reliques ", a writer in the " Gentleman's Magazine," 1775, pointed out that the locality of the ballad was not " the house of Rhodes," but " the house of Towie ", and referred him to the incident as given by Spottiswood in his " History of the Church of Scotland." The incident occurred, November 1571, during the conflict between the partisans of Queen Mary and the supporters of the Regency or King's party—the Gordons adhering to the Queen's, and the Forbeses to the King's side. After the home of the ballad got definitely fixed in Aberdeenshire, it was discovered that among contemporary authorities, while the majority located the incident at " the house of Towie," one, and that a local writer, gave it as having taken place at the Castle of Corgarff. The strictly contemporary documents (one of them written by a strong partisan of the Queen's or Gordon party) which gave the " Castle," or " house of Towie " as the scene of the burning, are : 1. *The Diurnall of Occurrents* (p. 255), where it is recorded that " Adam Gordon sent Captain Ker to the house of Toway, requesting the lady to surrender the place of Carrigill to him in the Queen's name "—which being refused—he burned the house with the lady and some 27 inmates therein. Whatever may be meant by " Carrigill," it was Towie which the writer says was burned. It possibly stands for Corriehoul, the largest and most valuable of various places on upper Donside held by Forbes of Towie as vassal of Lord Elphinstone, and which was, in due time, recovered from the Forbeses after the legitimate proprietor Lord Erskine had been restored to the Earldom of Mar by Queen Mary. 2. *The Historie of James the Sext* (p. 95), says, (Gordon) " directed his soldiers to the Castle of Towie and the lady thereof, refusing submission to his demands,—' he put fire to the house ' and burned herself and some 27, or thereby, inmates. 3. *Richard Bannantyne's Journal*, (p. 302), mentions similar circumstances, how the Gordons " went to the house of Towie "—and being refused—" laid the corns, hathe, and timber about it and set all on fire." All these are recognised works of high authority on the history of the period with which they deal. The strictly contemporary authority which places the incident at the Castle of Corgarff, is a manuscript genealogy, 1580, of the House of Forbes, by Mathew Lumsden, which was edited and brought down to date by William Forbes in 1667. It was printed at Inverness in 1819, and reprinted there in 1883. In enumerating the descendants of John Forbes of Towie (p. 54-55) by his wife Margaret Campbell—the writer says " the rest of ye sd Margaret Campbells bairns, with herself, were unmercifully murdered in the castle of Corgarffe." We have now no means however for determining the nature and extent of Forbes' editorial work on Lumsden's text ; and as Professor Child says, " we may owe Corgarff to the reviser of 1667, although he professes not to have altered the substance of his predecessor's work." In the whole circumstances we think the balance of evidence from contemporary writers is decidedly in favour of Towie, as the scene of the burning so graphically embodied in the ballad of Edom o Gordon.—Music : " Chappell Music of the Olden Time," p. 226 ; " Christie's Ballad Airs," I. p. 56.

GLENKINDIE.

1. Glenkindie was ance a harper gude,
   He harped to the king ;
   And Glenkindie was ance the best harper
   That ever harped on a string.

2. He'd harpit a fish out o' saut water,
   Or water out o' a stane ;
   Or milk out o' a maiden's breast,
   That bairn had never nane.

3. He's taen his harp intil his hand,
   He harpit and he sang ;
   And ay as he harpit to the king,
   To haud him unthought lang.

4. 'I'll gie you a robe, Glenkindie,
   A robe o' the royal pa',
   Gin ye will harp i' the winter's night
   Afore my nobles a'.'

5. And the king but and his nobles a',
   Sat birling at the wine ;
   And he wad hae but his ae dochter,
   To wait on them at dine.

6. He's taen his harp intil his hand,
   He's harpit them a' asleep,
   Except it was the young countess
   That love did waukin keep.

7. And first he has harpit a grave tune,
   And syne he has harpit a gay ;
   And mony a sich atween hands
   I wat the lady gae.

8. Says, 'Whan day is dawen, and cocks hae crawen,
   And wappit their wings sae wide,
   It's ye may come to my bower door,
   And streek you by my side.

9. 'But look that ye tell na Gib your man,
   For naething that ye dee ;
   For, an you tell him, Gib your man,
   He'll beguile baith you and me.'

10. He's taen his harp intil his hand ;
    He harpit and he sang ;
    And he is hame to Gib his man,
    As fast as he could gang.

11. 'O mith I tell you, Gib, my man,
    Gin I a man had slain ?'
    'O that ye micht, my gude master,
    Altho' ye had slain ten.'

12. 'Then tak ye tent now, Gib, my man,
        My bidden for to dee ;
    And, but an ye waukin me in time
        Ye sall be hangit hie.

13. 'When day has dawen, and cocks hae crawen,
        And wappit their wings sae wide,
    I'm bidden gang till yon lady's bower,
        And streek me by her side.'

14. 'Gae hame to your bed, my good master ;
        Ye've waukit, I fear, o'er lang ;
    For I'll wauken you in as good time,
        As ony cock i' the land.'

15. He's taen his harp intill his hand,
        He harpit and he sang,
    Until he harpit his master asleep,
        Syne fast awa did gang.

16. And he is till that lady's bower,
        As fast as he could rin ;
    When he cam to that lady's bower,
        He chappit at the chin.

17. 'O wha is this,' says that lady,
        'That opens nae and comes in ? '
    'It's I, Glenkindie, your ain true love,
        O, open and lat me in !'

18. She kent he was nae gentle knicht
        That she had latten in ;
    For neither when he gaed nor cam,
        Kist he her cheek or chin.

19. He neither kist her when he cam,
        Nor clappit her when he gaed ;
    And in and at her bower window,
        The moon shone like the gleed.

20. 'O ragged is your hose, Glenkindie,
        And riven is your sheen,
    And reavel'd is your yellow hair
        That I saw late yestreen.'

21. 'The stockings they are Gib my man's,
        They came first to my hand ;
    And this is Gib my man's shoon ;
        At my bed feet they stand.
    I've reavell'd a' my yellow hair
        Coming against the wind.'

22. He's taen the harp intill his hand,
        He harpit and he sang,
    Until he cam to his master,
        As fast as he could gang.

23. 'Won up, won up, my good master;
     I fear ye sleep o'er lang;
There's nae a cock in a' the land
     But has wappit his wings and crawn.'

24. Glenkindie's tane his harp in hand;
     He harpit and he sang,
And he has reached the lady's bower,
     Afore that e'er he blan.

25. When he came to the lady's bower,
     He chappit at the chin;
'O, wha is that at my bower door,
     That opens na and comes in?'
'It's I, Glenkindie, your ain true love,
     And in I canna win!'

    *   *   *   *   *

26. 'Forbid it, forbid it,' says that lady,
     'That ever sic shame betide;
That I should first be a wild loon's lass,
     And then a young knight's bride.'

27. There was nae pity for that lady,
     For she lay cald and dead;
But a' was for him, Glenkindie,
     In bower he must go mad.

28. He'd harpit a fish out o' saut water;
     The water out o' a stane;
The milk out o' a maiden's breast,
     That bairn had never nane.

29. He's taen his harp intil his hand;
     Sae sweetly as it rang,
And wae and weary was to hear
     Glenkindie's dowie sang.

30. But cald and dead was that lady,
     Nor heeds for a' his maen;
And he had harpit till domisday
     She'll never speak again.

31. He's taen his harp intill his hand;
     He harpit and he sang;
And he is hame to Gib his man
     As fast as he could gang.

32. Come forth, come forth, now, Gib, my man,
     Till I pay you your fee;
Come forth, come forth, now, Gib, my man,
     Weel payit sall ye be!'

33. And he has taen him, Gib, his man,
    And he has hang'd him hie ;
    And he's hangit him o'er his ain yate
    As high as high could be.*

IX.—STRATHDON.

O heather hills and marbled skies,
Whose lovely beauty fills mine eyes,
Yours are the charms, untouched by art,
At once to captivate the heart.
While mid your solitudes I stray
From man and misery far away,
Sin and its sorrows disappear,
I have no grief, I feel no fear,
But, rising from the mountain sod,
My happy spirit blesses God !

STRATHDON seems a more appropriate name for the whole valley of the river than for its·uppermost parish, but it is useless now to find fault with the nomenclature. It was originally known as Invernochty, probably from the principal church of the parish having stood at the confluence of the Nochty with the Don ; but neither of the names is particularly appropriate. Since we entered the "Highlands" of Donside, the valley has lost its "strath-like" appearance ; the bounding hills have approached nearer the banks of the river, and cultivation is therefore confined to narrow belts ; while the windings of the Don and its guardian hills restrict the view very considerably, so that latterly our walk affords a series of pleasant scenery surprises. Moreover, as we advance Westward we have lateral glens right and left, picturesque breaks in the landscape. The remoteness and comparative inaccessibility of Strathdon seem to impress themselves on the visitor who has penetrated to this secluded region, and which a superficial observer might credit with having little mutual intercourse with the world beyond its own hills. Yet many of the names of the

---

* From Jamieson's "Popular Ballads and Songs" 1806 (Vol I. p. 93). It is the earliest Scottish version of a ballad presumably of Welsh origin and of considerable antiquity, the hero, Glaskirion, being a famous bard and harper mentioned by Chaucer and other early writers. The earliest copy extant is an English one— "Glasgerion "—contained in the Percy Folio Manuscript (a slightly emmended text of which was given by Percy in the " Reliques ") and in which " Jacke my boy " takes the place of the Scottish " Gib, my man." The version we have printed has been tinkered by Jamieson, who received his copy from Professor Scott of Aberdeen "taken down from the recitation of an old woman ;" but not pleased with this, Jamieson "slightly improved" it by the incorporation of "a fragment communicated by the Rev. William Gray of Lincoln." In the Kinloch MSS. there is a version in the hand-writing of John Hill Burton, but it is of little value.

No circumstance connected with any of the families who have owned Glenkindie has ever been suggested for the story of the ballad, though it has long been a local favourite. For references to the mysterious power of the harp recognised in the ballad and folk-lore of other countries, see "Child's English and Scottish Popular Ballads," II. p. 137.

places and individuals in the next paragraph seem to have a familiar sound, and we claim acquaintance with them from their associations with the past. The inhabitants of Strathdon, gentle and simple, have of old done the state some service, and there are no symptoms of decay in the present day.

The principal estates, with their owners, in Strathdon are :— Allargue, Captain D. L. W. Farquharson ; Auchernach, W. N. Forbes ; Candacraig, Newe, Skellater, and Edinglassie, Sir Charles S. Forbes, Bart. ; Glenkindie, Alexander H. Leith ; Glen Nochty, Trustees of the late Henry Burra ; Invernettie, Trustees of the late Rev. John Watt ; Rhinstock, Major Fraser ; Belnabodach, Francis Farquharson ; Inverernan, General Sir John Forbes, G.C.B. ; and Delnadamph, John J. Mowbray.

According to "The New Statistical Account" the proprietors of machinery in the lower part of the Don contemplated building three extensive reservoirs in the parish of Strathdon for a constant and regular supply of water. One of these reservoirs was to be constructed at "the head of the Don", the second on the Nochty, and the third on the Deskry. Surveys were made, but the project was abandoned.

Leaving Bridge of Bucket Castle Newe, nearly three miles to the South-west, is the first object of interest. It stands at an altitude of 898 feet above sea level on the Southern slope of the mountain whose name it bears. The public road formerly passed in front of the castle on the left bank of the river, but was diverted for some distance to the other side for the sake of privacy. Bridge of Buchaam at the East end of the castle grounds and Bridge of Newe at the West are the bridges which had to be erected in 1858 for this purpose. Between these bridges we cross the Deskry Water, and pass on the left the little hamlet of Heugh-head with its old Market Stance. There is a fine specimen of an Eirde House near the Bridge of Buchaam in which were found "the following relics of human occupation—an iron ring, and an object of iron which looked like the shoe of a wooden spade, some staves of a wooden cog, a wooden comb, some fragments of pottery of coarse workmanship, a portion of a quern or handmill for grinding grain, fragments of deer's horns, and bones of the sheep and common domestic fowls".

Castle Newe.

The old house of Newe was erected in 1604, and has been skilfully inwrought with a modern castellated addition in 1831, whereby it was converted into one of the very finest residences on Donside. The central tower is 85 feet in height. The architect was the famous Archibald Simpson, and the material used was Kildrummy freestone. Notwithstanding its altitude the castle is sheltered by many fine trees, including ash, elm, scyamore, birch and rowan ; even oaks thrive there, while there are, of course, numerous Scottish firs. The principal entrance is guarded by two miniature cannon with "Lonach" engraved on them.

Castle Neave

John Forbes of Newe, who died in 1821, left £10,000 for the building of the new Lunatic Asylum in Aberdeen, and his nephew and successor, Sir Charles Forbes, Bart., paid the legacy duty, £1000, thereon. A handsome and conspicuous obelisk, in the Asylum grounds, was erected in honour of uncle and nephew by, as it bears, "public subscriptions, limited in amount to two guineas each, by the inhabitants of the city and county of Aberdeen".

Colquhonny Castle (18¾ miles from Alford) stands a little to the West of Castle Newe. The ruins consist of a vaulted storey of a tower, said to have been commenced by Forbes of Towie in the sixteenth century, but never finished. On the brae alongside it are Lonach Hall and a comfortable Hotel. The Lonach Highland and Friendly Society was established in 1825 pretty much on the same lines as the Braemar Royal Highland Society. The annual games held under its auspices are exceedingly popular, both in and beyond the district.

Forbestown, a little hamlet, is close on the West to Colquhonny Castle, near the 44th milestone. A very short distance farther Westward is Bellabeg, close to the Water of Nochty where that stream is crossed by the road ; on the other side of Nochty is the Doune of Invernochty. On the South side of the Don, opposite Bellabeg, the church of Strathdon with its handsome spire is a conspicuous object. The scenery in the neighbourhood of the church is very fine ; the glen is narrow, and the winding river is closely confined by wooded hills.

The church of Invernochty was granted by the Earl of Mar, 1199-1207, to the Priory of Monymusk ; in 1256 it became a prebend of S. Machar Cathedral. An old church, dating from 1757, was demolished in 1851, and the present handsome edifice erected on the site. There is an ambitious mausoleum at the principal entrance, the lower part of which served on our last visit as a board for advertising sales of turnips, &c. On the monument recording the death in 1698 of William Forbes, said to have been the first of that name of Newe, are the following lines :—

> Remember man, as thou goes by,
> As thou art now, so once was I ;
> As I am now, so must thou be ;
> Remember man that thou must die.

"There was a good carved fir pew in Strathdon church containing five carved panels, on three of which were the armorial bearings of the Elphinstone of Bellabeg and the Forbes of Skellater families. It is not very early in date, because, though one panel has the year 1597 cut on it, it is exactly in the same style and has the identical ornamentation of the others, which are dated 1636 and 1686. On the style below three of the panels are the mottoes plainly carved, 'Dum spiro spero', 'Sat amico te mihi fac'".—(Sir James Balfour Paul's "Heraldry in Relation to Art", 1900).

The Doune of Invernochty is an oval flat-topped mound, about 60 feet in height, of the same class as that of the Bass at Inverurie. It had been artificially altered and thereafter fortified at some remote period, and surrounded by a moat 26 feet wide and 16 feet deep. The circumference at the base is 970 feet, and at the top 562 feet, where there is an area of about half an acre. Traces of buildings are still visible on the top. There was water in the moat so recently as 1823 when the new turnpike was made ; the supply came from a little streamlet dignified with the name of the *River* Bardoch.

Bridge of Nochty reminds us that though we are in the Highlands there is no lack of indications of civilization—for at

Glen Nochty.

Bellabeg there is a branch bank office, a shop, and a direction post. Here also the Donside coaches start on their way to Gartly and Alford. The direction post gives the following distances : Invernettie, 1¾ miles ; Auchernach, 2½ miles ; Glenbucket Lodge, 4¼ miles. Invernettie and Auchernach are up Glen Nochty, the former on the right bank of Nettie Burn, the latter near the confluence of the Burn of Rhinstock with the Nochty. Auchernach House was built in 1809, and was long reputed the best in the district. It contains a collection of ancient and modern armour. A tablet on the South wall of Strathdon church records the death in 1794 of "Charles Forbes of Auchernach who lies here with his forefathers for upwards of 200 years". This Charles Forbes was barrackmaster of Corgarff Castle ; a son rose to be a Lieutenant-General in India. Glen Nochty is rather bare, and cultivation is a continual struggle with the elements, as may be gathered from the following experience. Descending towards Auchernach we had an exceedingly pleasant "crack" with a farmer whom we found a very intelligent man, not without a spice of humour. Asking him how he managed to get through a bad season, he said— "Weel, we jist manage to warstle through't somehow", and then he added, with a genial laugh—"Ye see, it's a warstle even in a good season, and a bad season disna mak' the warstle muckle waur !"

John Milne, the wandering minstrel "o' Livet's Glen", has immortalised Glen Nochty and its fighting smugglers in his poem of "Nochty Glens", which forms the *piece de resistance* in his "Songs and Poems", 1871.

Resuming our Westward walk from Bellabeg, which by the way was formerly known as Ballebeg (Little Town), and passing the Doune we have, near the 45th milestone, the well-known Bridge of Pooldhulie. It consists of a single arch of 70 feet span, crossing the Don a few yards above Pooldhulie Pot, where the river forms one of its smaller "crooks". It was built in 1715 by John Forbes of Inverernan, and was one of the few bridges over the Don that withstood uninjured the 1829 flood. This bridge connects the main road on the left bank of the Don with the old turnpike on the right bank.

Shortly after passing the 45th milestone we have, close on the left, a little conical mound known as Seely Hillock, a mythical residence of the fairies, which recalls Seely Howe in Logie-Coldstone. On the opposite side of the road, a few yards farther Westward, is the little hamlet of Parkvilla, formerly called Roughpark ; like Forbestown, it stands on the North side of the road. Morven from this neighbourhood looks particularly grand, while the huge " nose " of Ben Newe is a striking object to the Eastward.

Candacraig House, a mixture of the Elizabethan and the Scottish manor house styles, dates from 1835. It stands among trees between the road and the river, near the 46th milestone. The estate of Candacraig long belonged to the Andersons, as testified by inscriptions on tablets within the church of Strathdon. The tablet to the memory of the tenth laird of that name was erected by his widow in 1835 ; she was a daughter of the fourth Duke of Gordon by his second wife, Jean Christie.

> Smooth-winding Carvie trace thro' fertile ground,
> Famed for the various eels that there abound.

The Water of Carvie enters the Don about half a mile to the East of Candacraig. Near the confluence at Tomanchapel, is the supposed site of an old chapel. The Water of Carvie rises in the Slacks of Glencarvie, between Mullachdubh (2233 feet) and Allt a' Bhreabadair Hill (2456 feet). The Slacks is a deep, narrow, rocky gorge, forming a prominent " window " on the horizon. At the upper end there is a detached rock known as Castle Wilson, which a noted freebooter of that name was accustomed to use as a shelter. There is a fine view from this point of Lonach Hill, Glen Ernan, Glen Nochty, and The Buck. The Forest of Bunzeach lies between Glen Carvie and Deskry Water ; it is probably called a " forest " because several landowners have grazing and fuel rights over it.

Deskry Water, which pays its tribute to the Don about half a mile to the East of Castle Newe, rises near the summit of Morven (2862 feet), a mountain which has been for some time in our excursion the predominating feature in the landscape, and the barrier between us and Deeside. Boltinstone is a small hostel, of old familiar to drovers, on the right bank of the Deskry. A direction post there gives the following distances :—

Miles.		Miles.	
2½	Donside Road.	3⅝	Bridge of Towie.
7½	Tarland.	2	Heugh-head.
9⅝	Dinnet Station.		

The view from the Blue Cairn of Morven, as the summit is called, may be briefly given : Eastward, the smoke of Aberdeen can be seen, and Bennachie, Tap o' Noth, The Buck, Mormond Hill, and the Binn of Cullen are easily distinguishable ; to the West are Ben Avon and Beinn a' Bhuird, with the Central Cairngorms towering behind them. The Southward prospect is perhaps the most impressive, for there we have " the steep frowning glories of dark Lochnagar ", and Mount Keen with its beautiful cone-shaped top standing out clear against the sky. To the South-east are Mount Battock, Clochnaben, Kerloch, and Cairn-mon-earn. The Queen climbed Morven on 14th September, 1859, and wrote of the view that it was "more magnificent than can be described, so large yet so near everything seemed, and such seas of mountains with blue lights, and the colours so wonderfully beautiful . . . . it was enchanting"!

> Taught by their sires to bend the bow
> On Ernan's dark, dark hills of wind,
> The boys in childhood chased the roe,
> And left their hounds in speed behind.

Leaving Candacraig behind, we are struck with the view of Inverernan and Lonach Hill. Indeed Inverernan is as fine as anything on Deeside ; the house is an old **Glen Ernan.** building, but with extensive modern additions, charmingly situated among plantations near the mouth of Ernan Water. The district of Corgarff is entered at Inverernan. The first Forbes of Inverernan was "Black Jock", with whom we are familiar as having been Baillie to the Earl of Mar in 1715. The Earl's letter to him in connection with the Rising of that year may appropriately enough be given here :—

Invercauld,

Sept. 9 (at night) 1715.

JOCKE,—Ye was right not to come with the hundred men ye sent up to-night, when I expected four times that number. It is a pretty thing, when all the Highlands of Scotland are now rising upon the King and the country's account, as I have accounts from them since they were with me, and the gentlemen of the neighbouring Lowlands expecting us down to join them, that my men should only be refractory. Is not this the thing we are now about which they have been wishing these twenty-six years? And now, when it is come, and the King and the country's cause is at stake, will they for ever sit still and see all perish? I have used gentle means too long, and shall be forced to put other means into execution. I have sent you enclosed an order for the Lordship of Kildrummy, which you are immediately to intimate to all my vassals ; if they give ready obedience, it will make some amends, and if not, ye may tell them from me, that it will not be in my power to save them (were I willing) from being treated as enemies by those who are ready soon to join me ; and they may depend on it that I will be the first to propose and order their being so. Particularly let my own tenants in Kildrummy know that if they come not forth with their best arms, that I will send a party immediately to burn what they shall miss taking from them. And they may believe this only a threat, but by all that's sacred, I'll put it into execution, let my loss be what it will, that it may be an example to others. You are to tell the gentlemen that I'll expect them in their best accoutrements, on horseback, and no excuse to be accepted of. Go about this with diligence, and come yourself, and let me know your having done so. All this is not only as ye will be answerable to me, but to your King and country.

Your assured friend and servant,

MAR.

To John Forbes of Inveran,
Baillie of Kildrummy.

John Forbes himself bore his part and was taken prisoner. He died in Carlisle the night previous to the day fixed for his execution.

Ernan Water rises on the Banffshire boundary, between Meikle Corr Riabhach (2553 feet) and Carn Liath (2598 feet). Glen Ernan is even less cultivated than its parallel glens—Bucket and Nochty. " Don " is responsible for the following statement : here "the deer are to be seen in great numbers ; but for a person to kill any of them is a capital crime, though they destroy the corn in that neighbourhood ". But as the glen is not in a deer forest, any deer seen there are wanderers, and there is little corn now to be eaten up by them. The house of Edinglassie, now occupied as a shooting box, is about a mile up the glen, on the left bank of the Water, on the Southern slopes of Breagach Hill (1825 feet). There are a Rookery and a Heronry here.

On the West side of Glen Ernan, opposite Edinglassie, is Carn Mor, the lower part of which, within a loop of the Don, is called Lonach Hill. The highest point (1892 feet) has a large cairn, erected in 1823, with inscriptions in Gaelic and English. The latter is as follows : " Baronet's Cairn. The Tenantry on the lands of Newe, Edinglassie, Bellabeg, and Skellater, in testimony of their affection and gratitude, have erected this pile to their highly distingushed and beloved landlord, Sir Charles Forbes, Bart., M.P., on his elevation to the dignity of a Baronet of the United Kingdom, by His Majesty George IV., in 1823 ".

> By silver streams, where purling Don takes rise,
> Beneath a mountain tow'ring to the skies,
> Where crystal brooks in gentle murmurs glide
> From neighb'ring hills and swell their sov'reign's tide.

Again taking the Westward road and leaving Inverernan behind we pass, close to the 47th milestone, Forbes Lodge, a small house with a fine situation. Nearly opposite, Conrie Water, which rises between Allt a' Bhreabadair Hill and Meikle Sgroilleach Hill (2432 feet), joins the Don. **Corgarff.** The summit of the latter hill is about a mile to the East of the

old military road between Crathie and Corgarff, which here
crosses the watershed at a height of about 1800 feet.

This road leaves Glen Gairn at Gairnshiel and, striking into
the head of Glen Finzie by Allt Glaschoille, descends on Donside, crossing the Burn of Tornahaish about three-quarters of a
mile above the Roman Catholic chapel, and crossing the Don
at Bridge-end of Allargue. Sgroilleach is a rather flat, humpy
hill, partaking much of the nature of the watershed ridge from
Meikle Geal Charn to Morven, the boundary between the
parishes of Glenmuick-Tullich-Glengairn and Strathdon. Peats
are still cut on both the North and South sides almost to the
very top, where quartz crops out. The view includes Glen
Finzie, Mount Keen, Glen Muick, the Coyles, Capel Mounth,
Conachcraig, Lochnagar, and the hills Westward on the
South side of the Dee to the head of Glen Ey, Brown
Cow Hill, the Craigandals, Beinn a' Bhuird—the top
of the Eastern corries being seen over Ben Avon—Ben Avon,
Ben Bynac (?), Meall na Gaineimh, the Don about Cock Bridge,
Allargue, Corgarff church, Lonach Hill, The Buck, Tap o'
North, Ben Newe, Bennachie, Morven, Kerloch, Clochnaben,
and Mount Battock. Descending a little towards Little
Sgroilleach Hill (on the North) Inverernan will be seen. The
graceful outline of The Buck relieves the rather monotonous
and featureless ridge on the North side of the Don, Ben Newe
alone standing out boldly with its distinctive peak among the
upper Donside hills. The Mither Tap and the Millstone Hill
are the prominent summits of the " grey king of common hills ".
Morven, as usual, shuts out a very considerable portion of the
Eastward scene, and "the stone" of Clochnaben is under the
horizon. Allt a' Bhreabadair Hill on the East, and Carn a'
Bhacain (2442 feet) on the West, are the immediate neighbours
of Sgroilleach, and from their proximity and slightly greater
elevation, restrict the prospect. On the 27th October the cone
of Mount Keen was white, while in Corgarff the scythe was
seen at work.

Resuming our journey we pass, in rounding the Southern
slope of pine-clad Lonach Hill, another small house, now known
as Lonach Lodge, on the roadside, at an altitude of 1050 feet.
The house is quite shut in by hills and trees. A little to the
North-westward, on the right bank of the Don, is Delhandy,
where there is a slight eminence within a "crook" of the Don.
It formerly belonged to the Skellater family, one of which,
Nathaniel Forbes of Delhandy, was an officer in the Earl of
Mar's Donside corps in the '15. In a contest at putting the
stone he is said to have so stretched the muscles of his legs
that his garters burst in three pieces.

Skellater is an old mansion near the 48th milestone, on the
Southern slope of Lonach Hill. It lies in a pine-clothed corrie,
and has a beautiful situation ; here one can see little of the
valley to the East on account of the pleasant windings of the
river. John Forbes of Skellater married a Portuguese princess,

and became a Field Marshal in the Portuguese army. In 1809 he died in Brazil, whither he had accompanied the royal family.

Tom Fuaraich (1840 feet) is on the right bank of the Don, opposite Skellater. At Ord, near the river, on the North of Tom Fuariach, there is the site of a chapel ; on the West side of the hill, at a height of about 1600 feet, a remarkable discovery was made in 1822 while digging the foundation of a dyke. Several hundred silver coins and two rings were found. The coins were nearly all of the reign of Henry III., some of them of William the Lion, and two of King John. One of the rings was of gold with a small dark sapphire ; a similar ring was discovered in 1829 in the cathedral of Chichester, in the coffin of a Bishop of that city, who had died in 1146. The other was a broken iron gilt ring with a pale sapphire, and similiar to many Arabian and Indian rings. According to "The Donean Tourist" there was a previous "find" here. "On this hill are two pretty large tumuli ; one of them called the Watch Craig, where a party of the 42nd Regiment was stationed, to suppress the Kern Marauders, this being their rendezvous : the other is called Cairn Fioul, the place where they divided the spoil taken on their *raid*. In 1694 were found many pieces of silver, which were claimed by the family of Skellater, and defaced to make household plate. Some of the pieces were dollars of Charles II., valued at 56 shillings, milled money".

Skellater left behind, the indications that our journey is nearing an end increase step by step. At Garchory, however, near the 49th milestone, there are a corn mill and a grocer's shop, at Colnabachin, near the 50th milestone, there in a struggling hamlet, where the Don is crossed by a foot-bridge, at the ford of Tornahaish, in connection with the Deeside road (page 120). The Burn of Tornahaish rises on Carn a' Bhacain, and gives its name to a small hamlet near its confluence with the Don. On the left bank, between the burn and the Don, is Hill of Tornahaish (1494 feet), with, on the summit, a cairn erected by the natives in memory of John Forbes of Newe.

Anciently there had been two places of worship in Corgarff —the nameless chapel at Ord, and S. Machar Chapel at Corriehoul, on the East bank of Allt Coire Tholl, at the 51st milestone, the latter unquestionably the more important. A legend connected with a well still known as Tobar Machar, or Machar's Well, in its immediate neighbohrhood is rather interesting. Corgarff was on a certain occasion suffering from a famine, doubtless no uncommon occurrence in old times in that district. The people were in great distress from lack of food ; even the priest's larder was absolutely empty. His troubled housekeeper, at her wit's end, could only report the circumstances to his reverence, as she knew his flock were in equally dire straits. The priest, after listening quietly to Martha's wail, stepped across to the well, where he knelt and prayed to S. Machar for food, not only for himself, but for his starving parishioners. Returning to the house he told his housekeeper to go to the well at sunrise and, without looking into it, walk three times round in the name of the Trinity, and thereafter draw a draught of water. Carefully carrying out her instructions she dipped in her pail and brought up three salmon! The operation was repeated as often as necessary till relief came in the ordinary course to the famine-stricken people.

Corriehoul has, in addition to the site of S. Machar's Chapel, a grave-yard which, as an old writer says, "is still used for burying many of the people in Corgarff, and all the soldiers who die in the Castle are interred there with all the ceremonies that are used in the army, but its appearance is very odd like, as there is no dyke about the graves, and from its lying remote from any house, in an open field". This reproach seems to have ultimately produced an effect, for the Churchyard is now surrounded by a modest wall, the gate bearing the inscription :—" The people of Corgarff erected this gate and wall ".

The church of Corgarff is in the vicinity of the grave-yard. "On the Northern verge of the Don is the supplementary Church at Lynn Oarn, erected for a chaplain, while the soldiers occupied the garrison, but owing to the longitude of the parish of Strathdon, they are proposing to form it into a separate parish".—(" The Donean Tourist "). Lynn Oarn, now Loinorne, is the name of a small croft at the church of Corgarff. A short distance beyond the church we reach the Corgarff Post Office at Greenbank, near the 52nd and last milestone ; and thereafter cross the Don by Luib Bridge, at an altitude of 1285 feet above sea level.

There is a Kelpy legend concerning a former bridge of Luib, which was a wooden erection. The story has it that a man had to cross it in order to get to his wife who was then very ill. When he reached the river he found that the bridge had been swept away by a flood, and as he was despairing of reaching the other bank a tall stranger suddenly appeared and offered to carry him across. The man was at first doubtful, but ultimately accepted the offer. When the couple reached the middle of the stream the Kelpy, hitherto so plausible, endeavoured to plunge with his burden beneath the water. The passenger, however, found a foothold, and, disengaging himself from the Kelpy, scrambled up the bank, followed by a boulder hurled by the disappointed water-spirit. The boulder became known as the Kelpy's Stone, and, as passers-by added stones to it, the Kelpy's Cairn.

Shortly after crossing Luib Bridge we find ourselves at the little hamlet of The Cock. Allt a' Choilich (Cock Burn), which is doubtless responsible for this name, rises between Brown Cow Hill and Camock Hill (2219 feet). Corgarff Castle is on the left bank of this burn, a short distance above its confluence ; the

Corgarff Castle

name Castletown, just below the castle, reminds us of its antiquity. The road crosses Cock Burn by " Cock Brig ", and, a few yards beyond, the Don is crossed by its uppermost bridge at Bridge-end of Allargue, where there is a convenient Inn. This Inn formerly stood at The Cock where " the people who kept the public house at the end of the Bridge, had for their sign a Red Cock painted and hung up, which made soldiers coming that way inquire for the Cock-bridge, which name it retains to this day ". Allargue House overlooks the Don from the North, near Bridge-end.

> 'Tis now the raven's black abode,
> 'Tis now the apartment of the toad,
> And there the fox securely feeds,
> And there the pois'nous adder breeds.

Corgarff Castle was originally a small oblong four storeyed tower with wings, to which various additions were made in comparatively recent times. Tradition says that it was built by the Earl of Mar as a hunting seat. Among other portions of this Earldom, James IV. granted the " Foresta de Corgarf" to Alexander Elphinstone. By the end of the 16th century, the most, if not all, of the lands of Corgarff had been acquired from the Lords Elphinstone by the Forbeses of Towie. On the 13th Jan., 1595, in an Inquest before the Sheriff of Aberdeen, for the service of Elizabeth Forbes, widow of Alexander Forbes of Towie, for her terce, the jury found that the said Alexander Forbes died "last vest and seized as of fee ", not only in the barony of Towie, but also in the lands of Easter and Wester Corriehoul, the Forest of Corgarff lying adjacent thereto, and in the "lands called Aulgarff". On the strength of the above, certain authorities have assumed that Corgarff Castle had been occupied in 1571 by John Forbes of Towie, father of the above Alexander Forbes, and was the place where his wife, family, and domestics were burned by Captain Ker. This subject has been much disputed by various writers, and a synopsis of the fundamental facts in the discussion will be found on p. 106 in a note to the ballad " Captain Car, or Edom o Gordon ".

Corgaff Castle.

In 1746 the castle was acquired by the Government as barracks to be used in connection with the disarming of the Highlanders, and the prevention of the " Depredations committed by these Villains and all the irregularities they are so remarkable for ". The following is an extract from a letter dated Aberdeen, 6th March, 1746, written by Captain Alexander Stuart to his brother, which will be found in Colonel Allardyce's " Historical Papers, 1699-1750," (New Spalding Club) :—

I returned on Wednesday from an expedition into the Highlands of Aberdeenshire, fifty miles from hence, to destroy a Magazine of the Rebels at Corgorff, which lies near the head of the Don. Three hundred foot commanded by Major Morris, and one hundred Dragoons commanded by me—the whole under the command of Lord Ancrum, were ordered for that duty. We marched from this on Friday, 28th February, in a snowy day to *Monimuss*, Sir Archibald Grant's house. Next day over mountains and Moors almost impassable at any time of the year, but much more so when covered with snow, to a place called Tarland. As soon as they saw us directing our march thither, they suspected our design on the Magazine there, and some Rebels who lived there sent away an Express immediately to acquaint the Garrison, and to Glenbucket, who was with some men at Glenlivet above Strathdon, about ten miles above the castle. On Saturday morning we marched from Tarland, a most terrible march, to the Castle, which stands on the side of the Don, where I daresay never Dragoons were before, nor ever will be again, nor foot neither, unless Highlanders ! Though we marched early in the morning it was past four before we arrived there. We found it abandoned by the Garrison, but so lately, that the fire was burning, and no living creature in the house but a poor cat sitting by the fire. They had thrown the barrels of powder down the bank into the river in order I suppose to destroy it, but had not time—and had conveyed the arms up and down the hills near it in different directions, and hid the bayonets under a dung-hill. However we found all out, and brought away 367 firelocks, 370 bayonets. There were some more arms destroyed, which we could not carry. Ten thousand musket balls we threw into the river and amongst the heather, &c., and it being impossible to convey away the powder for want of country horses, all gone to the hills with the country folks who had run away, being told by the rebels that we were to burn and destroy the whole country. We staved thirty-two double barrels of exceeding fine Spanish powder equal to sixty-nine of our barrels, and threw it all into the river—and afterwards, for want of horses were obliged to burn and destroy so many of the firelocks, that we brought but 131 to Aberdeen. We returned on Wednesday from such a country that a hundred men might beat a thousand from the hills above them—and had it snowed another night when we were there, it had been impossible to have returned. We were obliged to be two nights in the open fields —and sit on horseback all night. However we happily executed what we were sent upon—and, thank God, returned safe, with only the loss of one horse.

In " The Donean Tourist " the force sent against Corgarff Castle is magnified to 2000 men !

In April 1748, Colonel Watson " passed through Aberdeen *en route* to Corgarff to give directions for repairing the castle there" (*Aberdeen Journal*, 5th April, 1748) ; and it must have been then that the parapet and all the corbels on which the parapet rested, except the two that still remain over the door, were removed. Two plain gables were then built on the tower, with ordinary eighteenth century chimney tops ; the common sloping roof that now exists was put on from gable to gable to form the attic or garret storey ; the small windows on the South side of the tower were abolished, and the seven existing eighteenth century windows slapped out in their stead : the small unshapely staircase was built on to the walls at the South-east corner to give access to the attic floors ; the one storey addition of a single room, with eighteenth century chimney, was made at each end ; and the whole was surrounded with the loopholed curtain, with salients on each of its four fronts to defend the flanks—all as they now exist. The garrison seems to have consisted (in 1750), of forty privates, three corporals, and two sergeants, a lieutenant being in command. This force included outposts at Inchrory (9) and Braes of Abernethy (6) ; and a moving patrol (7). It was not till about the year 1831 that the Government ceased to use the castle, and men still living remember the red-coats being there. Strathdon, it should be mentioned, was long notorious for smuggling, and the services of the garrison were necessary for its suppression.

At Bridge-end the Lecht road leads Northward over the Hill of Allargue (1805 feet) to Kirkmichael and Tomintoul. It crosses the county march between Meikle Corr Riabhach and Beinn a' Chruinnach (2536 feet). The blind, the deaf, and the lame had better make a slight divergence to the left in the ascent, and visit Tobar Fuar, the Cold Well. It lies within the forkings of the Burn of Loinherry, and its three springs, which are close to each other, cured blindness, deafness, and lameness respectively. Such cures, however, were not gratuitous ; the guardian spirit, who lived under a boulder, expected gold from her visitors. She was supposed to keep her gains in a kettle under the boulder, hence known as the kettle stone. The hoard was pretty safe, for it was generally believed in the district that a terrible death would instantly follow any attempt at robbery. About 1840, however, a number of youths, in spite of warnings from their elders, set out with the necessary implements, and turned over the boulder, but alas, neither kettle nor gold was to be seen. " The New Statistical Account" credits the Burn of Loinherry with being nearly the same size at its source as at its mouth. Locally Tobar Fuar was regarded as being the second largest spring in Scotland, and its outflow sufficient to drive an ordinary mill wheel.

The Easterly head stream of the Burn of Loinherry almost touches the Lecht road near the county march. About a third of a mile short of the march, on the Eastern slope of Carn Mhic an Toisich, is the iron mine of Allargue, which, mainly owing to the cost of carriage, became disused in 1866, after two seasons' working. The mine is at an elevation of about 1930 feet above sea level, on the right bank of the Loinherry tributary, and near the Lecht road. Iron is plentiful on the Banffshire side of the hills, and is also to be found at the head of Glen Ernan and Glen Nochty. It is an odd coincidence that the ridge on the county march is known as Leac a' Ghobhainn.

Delnadamph Lodge is about two miles West from Cock Bridge, on the South side of the Don ; its sheltering plantations are the uppermost in the valley. Allt Bheannaich is a little further Westward ; its left bank has several *larachs*, as well as the most Westerly house in Donside, Inchmore (1510 feet) a shepherd's cottage. Opposite Inchmore, on the North side of

Allt Tuileach, is Tom Dunan (1778 feet), between which and
Bridge-end are several small farms, the last evidences of successful struggling with nature in Corgarff. We give their names,
from the East : Delahash and Loinherry, on the left and right
banks respectively of the Burn of Loinherry ; Badnabein ;
Dunfeal ; Dunanfiew and Deldunan on the left and right banks
respectively of Allt Dunain ; and East Dunnandubh, and West
Dunnandubh.

West of Delnadamph Lodge the road degenerates very
rapidly, and makes no pretension to be more than a drove road.
A short distance to the West of Inchmore another track makes
for Strathavon, crossing the young river at Ford of Culchathadh
(1469 feet) and entering Banffshire at The Eag (1931 feet).
The Corgarff drove road, however, holds Westward for Inchrory,
rounding Stron na Crois-araich of Carn Cuilchathaidh. Opposite
the " Stron ", on the left bank of the stream, is the Feith Well,
between Allt Clach Mheann and Allt Craig Meann, at a height
of about 1480 feet. Locally this well is considered to be in no
way inferior to those at Strathpeffer ; certainly it tastes quite as
disagreeably as any of them. Some have had visions of the
Feith Bhait with its sulphurous spring becoming a fashionable
resort. Before descending on Inchrory, and so making for
Speyside or Deeside, the traveller who has accompanied us so
far should walk up Allt an Mhicheil, and so see with his own
eyes the source of the Don. Coire Domhain, with its semicircular top, seems not unworthy of its name (deep) ; the bottom
of the corrie is flat, and covered with heath, grass and rush.
Here we come on the tiniest of little water-falls with a drop of
three feet ; Michael's Burn thus springs into life and action, its
narrow cut or channel *apparently* leading to the Avon. Who
was Michael? The *larachs* in the neighbourhood are silent,
and only indicate that in " the good old days " summering was
common on the hill-slopes of Corgarff.

EPPIE MORRIE.

1. Four-and-twenty Highland men
      Came a' from Carrie side
   To steal awa Eppie Morrie,
      Cause she would not be a bride.

2. Out it's came her mother,
      It was a moonlight night
   She could not see her daughter,
      Their swords they shin'd so bright.

3. ' Haud far awa' frae me, mother,
      Haud far awa' frae me ;
   There's not a man in a' Strathdon
      Shall wedded be with me.'

4. They have taken Eppie Morrie,
   And horse back bound her on,
 And then awa' to the minister,
   As fast as horse could gang.

5. He's taken out a pistol, and
   Set it to the minister's breast :
 ' Marry me, marry me, minister,
   Or else I'll be your priest.'

6. ' Haud far awa' frae me, good sir,
   Haud far awa' frae me ;
 For there's not a man in all Strathdon
   That shall married be with me.'

7. ' Haud far awa' frae me, Willie,
   Haud far awa' frae me ;
 For I darna avow to marry you,
   Except she's as willing as ye.'

8. They have taken Eppie Morrie,
   Since better could nae be,
 And they're awa' to Carrie side,
   As fast as horse could flee.

9. When mass was sung and bells were rung,
   And all were bound for bed,
 Then Willie and Eppie Morrie,
   In one bed they were laid.

10. ' Haud far awa' frae me, Willie,
    Haud far awa' frae me ;
 Before I'll lie in your bed,
    I'll try my strength with thee.'

11. She took the cap frae off her head,
    And threw it to the way,
 Said ' Ere I'll lie in your bed,
    I'll fight with you till day.'

12. Then early in the morning,
    Before her clothes were on,
 In came the maiden of Scallatter
    Gown and shirt alone.

13. 'Get up, get up, young woman,
        And drink the wine wi' me.'
    ' Ye might have called me maiden,
        I'm sure as leal as thee.'

    *   *   *   *   *

14. ' Haud far awa' frae me, lady,
        Haud far awa' frae me ;
    There's not a man in a' Strathdon
        The day shall wed wi' me.'

15. Soon in there came Belbordlane,
        With a pistol on every side,
    ' Come awa hame, Eppie Morrie,
        And there you'll be my bride.'

16. ' Go get me a horse, Willie,
        And get it like a man,
    And send me back to my mother,
        A maiden as I cam.'

17. 'The sun shines o'er the westlin hills ;
        By the light lamp of the moon,
    Just saddle your horse, young John Forsyth,
        And whistle, and I'll come soon.'*

---

* This is one of a small class of Scottish Ballads which deals with
"the kidnapping of women for compulsory marriage," a practice
which came down to comparatively recent times in Scotland. We
have ballads dealing with Glenlyon's stealing of "bonny Baby
Livingston" from Dundee ; of the abduction of "the Lady of Arngask"
by Graham of Bracko Castle [about 1736]; and of Robert Oig, (son of
Rob Roy) who in 1750 forcibly stole Jean Key from her house in
Edinbelly, Stirlingshire, and for which he was executed at Edinburgh,
in 1754.

No identification of the personage "Willie" who stole Eppie
Morrie has been obtained. The ballad was first printed by Maidment
in "A North Country Garland," 1824. We have omitted one verse,
and softened the expression in one line of two of the verses : rough
phrasing which appears also in one of the versions of "Rob Roy." It
has all the appearance of belonging to the early years of the eighteenth
century, but its form has been debased by passing through low mouths.

Cottage Industries.

INDEX

Dark figures (thus **77**) denote the page referring more particularly to the subject.